How To
Catch Crabs
By The Bushel!

By The Same Author

How To Write For The Outdoor Magazines
Part Time Cash For The Sportsman
Good Fishing Close To New York City
Good Fishing In The Catskills
Northeast Hunting Guide

How To Catch Crabs By The Bushel!

By Jim Capossela

Drawings by Robin Havill

NORTHEAST SPORTSMAN'S PRESS
TARRYTOWN, NEW YORK

STACKPOLE BOOKS
HARRISBURG, PENNSYLVANIA

First Printing 1981
Seventh Printing 1990 Revised

Library of Congress Cataloging In Publication Data

Capossela, Jim.
How to catch crabs by the bushel!

1. Crabbing – Atlantic Coast (U.S.) 2. Blue crabs. 3. Cookery (Crabs) I. Capossela, Josephine.
II. Title.
SH400.5.C7C36 1982 799.1′7 82-90080
ISBN 0-8117-4023-4

Recipes created, compiled and tested with the generous assistance of Josephine Capossela.

Published by Stackpole Books and Northeast Sportsman's Press

Distributed by Stackpole Books
Cameron & Kelker Streets
Harrisburg, Pennsylvania 17105

Printed in the United States of America
10-9-8-7

Introduction

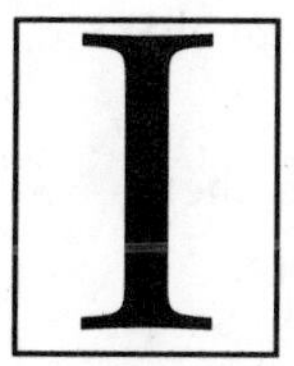

t's my sincere hope that this book will help you catch crabs by the bushel this season. But you'll get your money back after only about twelve crabs. Last summer, I saw big Jimmies (males) going for ten dollars a dozen! Even very small crabs were selling for five and six dollars for twelve. What better excuse for getting out and having fun catching them yourself.

Callinectes sapidus, the blue claw crab, provides more sport and more good eating than any other shellfish (or in fact any kind of fish) along the entire Atlantic Coast. The season is long. Licenses are usually not required. Take limits are liberal or nonexistent. Expensive, complicated gear is unnecessary. Anyone—male or female, young or old, can catch crabs.

To have the most fun though, and consistently catch a lot of crabs, takes an understanding of both where and when blue claws can be found. And it takes knowing which methods to use in which locations. Virtually nothing has been written about this subject for the noncommercial crabber. I hope this book will help to fill that void.

Sook - An adult female crab, after its final molt.

Jimmy - A male crab.

Buckram - Following papershell, a stage when a crab's shell has become slightly hard but is still pliable.

Peeler - A crab that is very close to "peeling" its outer shell (within a day or two) to become a softshell.

Shedder - Same thing as a peeler. Sometimes applied to a crab actually in the act of shedding its outer shell.

Sponge Crab - Female crab carrying an egg mass exposed around the abdomen.

Buster - A crab which is beginning to emerge from its old shell.

Softshell - A crab that has just emerged from its old shell, and now has a very soft, pliable new shell.

Sally - An immature female crab

Hardshell - A crab with a fully hardened shell. Usually within 4 days of shedding.

Buck and Rider - A large male crab "cradle carrying" a female, just prior to or after mating.

Keeper - A crab that is big enough to keep. Legally, this is often 5 inches.

Papershell - Following the softshell stage, a condition when the crab's shell has stiffened somewhat.

Red Sign - About the same as peeler.

Doublers - Same as buck and rider.

Pink Sign - A hard crab with about a week or less to go to moult.

White Sign - A hard crab with about two weeks or less to go to moult.

Channeler - A large male crab.

Snot or **Green** - Same as a white sign.

Contents

I should have been a pair
of ragged claws,

Scuttling across the floors
of silent seas.

T.S. Eliot

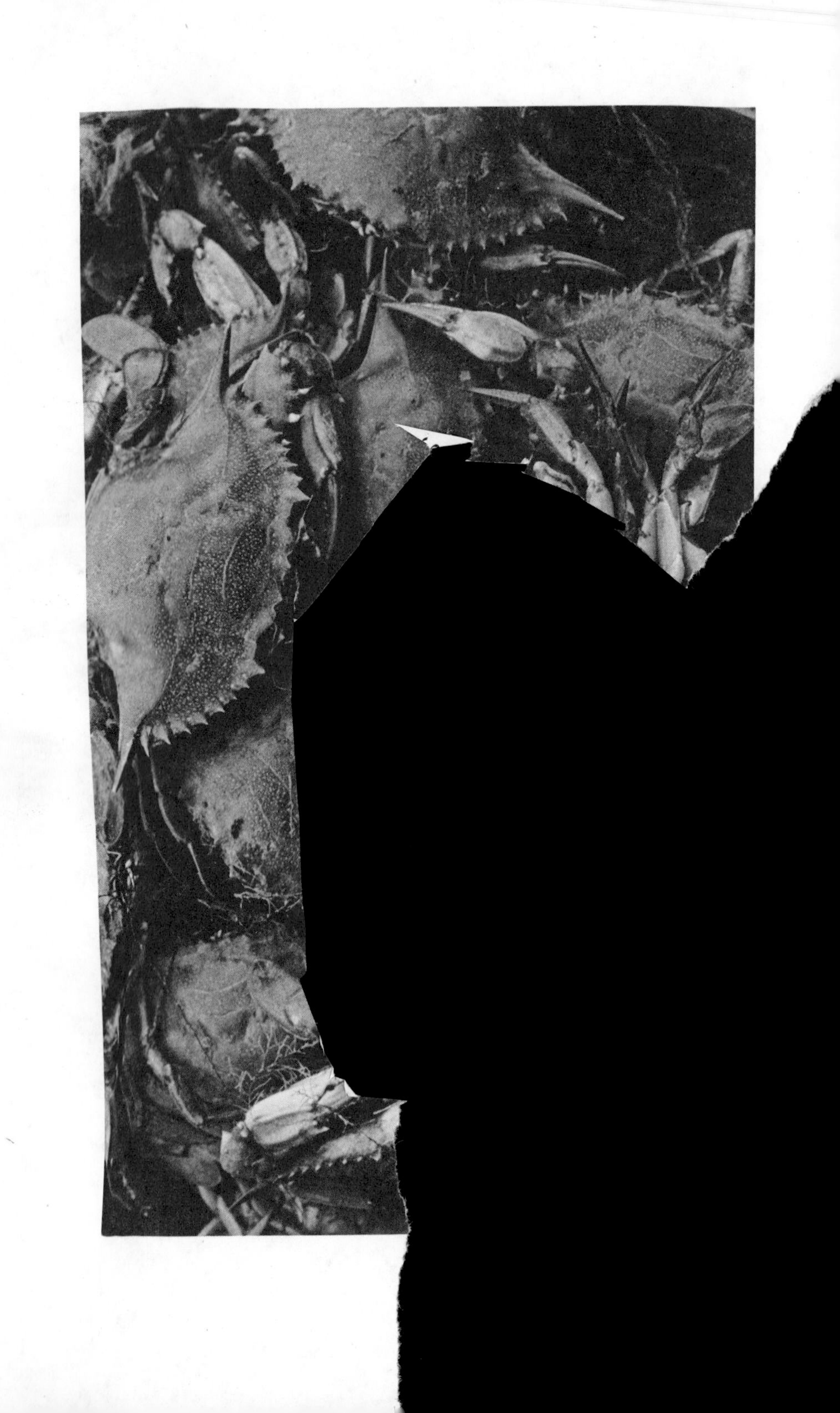

ONE

Secrets of the Mysterious Blue Claw

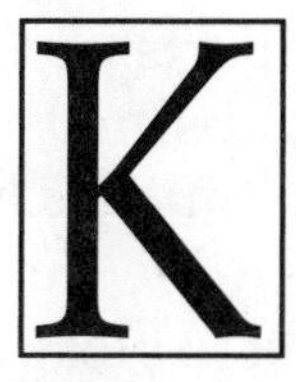

ingdom Animal, phylum Arthropoda, class Crustacea, family Portunidae, genus Callinectes, species sapidus: These are the terms scientists use to put him in his place. Yet if one were to snap in front of me a cue card that said "Blue Claw," the place that *my* mind would race to is a tidal bay where the osprey soars, the egret fishes, and the killie darts among the shallows. To many people—including most of the girlfriends in my history—it's a bug-infested swamp that stinks: literally at low tide, and figuratively at all times. But, to me, and to Charles Darwin, and to millions of other enlightened individuals, it's the most fascinating place in the world.

The blue claw crab is an arthropod, that group of animals having jointed legs and a segmented body. To get a little more particular, it is a crustacean, as are lobsters and shrimps. These fellows are known by their hard outer shell, jointed appendages and gills. Although the blue claw can live for many days out of the water, given the choice he pretty much stays in the water.

You measure him from "point to point," that is, between the tips of his lateral spines. In areas of high salinity, growth is retarded and a 5-incher may be a

We're fussy. But a 7 1/2-inch crab is a big crab in anybody's book. This jumbo male came from the mid Hudson estuary where salinities are fairly mild.

prime crab. In waters of middle salinity (10-24 parts per thousand salt; seawater is about 34), male crabs may grow to seven, eight and even, rarely, nine inches. Females seldom make it past six. Blue claws live an average of about 2 to 2 1/2 years, though some get to blow out three candles or even, occasionally, four. While in the hardshell stage, the blue crab is centurion of the marsh. But he must shed that protective shell in order to grow. Thus, some 25 to 30 times in his life, for about two days each, the blue claw is a helpless "softshell." Both man *and* many forms of beast relish this delicacy. Very small crabs shed every three to five days. Those 3 1/2 inches or bigger do it about every 20 to 50 days.

"Reading crabs" is one of the finest traditions of crabbing. Whether you're a commercial crabber or an amateur, this skill will enable you to dine on softshell crab far more often.

When a hard crab approaches a moult, a new shell begins to form inside the old one. Look at the next to last segment of the swimming leg. A faint outline of that new shell can be seen. If it appears whitish, it is a "white sign" crab with about 10-14 days to go to moult. If it's pinkish, it's a "pink sign" or "second" which will shed within about a week. If it's reddish, you have a "red sign" or "rank" crab that will moult within a day or two. If you can store your reds or even your pinks until they moult (see Ch. 5), you can obtain your own softshell crab.

Whenever you hear the excited cry, "the crabs are running!" you can be pretty sure it's blue claws they're talking about. No other crab even comes close to him, on the Atlantic coast, in terms of food, sport or commercial value. Great (though fluctuating) abundance, wide distribution, and savory meat make *Callinectes sapidus* second only to the shrimp among shellfish in dollar sales per year. For non-commercial sportsmen, the blue claw is number one along the Atlantic seaboard.

RANGE AND AVAILABILITY. Blue claws have been seen as far north as Nova Scotia. However, the primary range extends from Rhode Island south to Florida and the Gulf of Mexico. But the crab has now travelled to more exotic locales, too. Apparently via the ballast of U.S.A. ships, blue claws have made their way to the Mediterranean, and where Antony once swooned Cleopatra, Jimmies now swoon sooks: right in the Nile Delta! Back on our shores, the blue claw is widely available to sport crabbers from May to October between New Jersey and the Carolinas. In Georgia, Florida and the gulf states the season is longer; from Long Island northward, action may not develop until later in the spring.

LIFE CYCLE. Knowledge of the blue claw's intriguing life history will help you catch a lot more crabs, but more importantly, help you appreciate this marvelous animal all the better. Let us, then, briefly walk through both the seasons and stages of a blue claw's life.

Mainly between late spring and late summer, but also at other times, the abdomen of a mature female crab will begin to bulge with an egg mass of some 700,000 to 2 million eggs. This mass gradually turns from bright orange to yellow or brownish and then to blackish as the individual egg yolks are consumed. The lady at this point is appropriately named a "sponge crab," and must be returned in some states. When the eggs hatch, they are microscopic in size and become part of the planktonic or free-floating mass. They are called zoea larvae in this stage, and they look more like shrimp or insects than crabs. During the first tenuous months of existence—only a few of millions reach maturity—they actually pass into a post larval stage, or megalops. Then, after about seven moults, they begin to take on the general shape of an adult. Larval crabs are often swept en masse out into the ocean, but those that make it back into the estuary migrate towards markedly fresher water. Spring-spawned crabs may reach two inches by the end of their first summer, but will rarely turn up in the catch of sport crabbers.

Among the arthropods, blue crabs are the most cooperative in telling you their sex. Just examine the abdomen: At top is a male crab; in center is an immature female or "Sally"; at bottom is a mature female or "sook."

Blue crabs dig into the mud in winter, where they lie semi-dormant from about early December to late March. This is in the Chesapeake region. The further south you go, the shorter the dormancy period becomes, until only a sluggish period occurs in the warm gulf waters. North of the Chesapeake, the winter sojourn may be longer. These wintering crabs are not available to sport crabbers.

Crabs do not moult during winter dormancy, so the second spring sees our near one-year-old at about 2 1/2 inches. As summer wears on, he (or she) will moult several more times, and begin appearing in crab traps and on the ends of handlines. In the mid-Atlantic region, a high percentage of the actual mating is thought to occur in late summer. At this time, crabs may edge towards even fresher waters, 10 ppt. or less. Crabbers should definitely not exclude waters that border on being saltless at this time of year.

Males may mate several times, but females only once. The mature male, typically about 15 months old and five inches in length, will seek out a female of about the same age but a little smaller that is about to shed. (It should be noted that crabs hatched late, say September, may not mate until they are about 24 months old.) Properly, a female in this stage is called a peeler. There is an excellent reason for the male's choosiness in this regard: copulation and fertilization can only take place when the female has just shed.

The noble male or "Jimmy" picks up his chosen one, and holds her gently to him with his legs. This is called "cradle carrying." He will thus protect his beloved for a few days before and after copulation. At this time they are termed "doublers." They generally find a protected and secluded place in fairly shallow water, often in vegetation, for their one-time love affair. However, sport crabbers occasionally catch doublers in traps or with scap nets. If the female is still a "Sally", an immature female, the crabber can steal her—if he has the heart—and place her in a pail of water until she sheds out. Unless the event is just a few hours away, though, she will probably die of suffocation. Professional crabbers who market softshells keep peelers in outdoor "shedding floats" or indoor troughs till they actually bust out. Sport crabbers, without those devices, may have to buy most of their softshells at the fish store. There is more on softshell crabs in Ch. 5.

Our pair has mated and parted, and let us say it is now early October. Quickly after being fertilized, females will begin to migrate toward the ocean, often following shoals and bars, but staying in quite shallow water along the way. Before winter, many will end up in depths averaging 20 to 30 feet where salinities are about 25 ppt. or a little more. This is very often at the mouth of the estuary where they spent the summer. Mature males, and probably immature males and females, are known to slowly ease into deeper water as winter approaches. They may end up in the deepest holes and river channels of estuaries actually adjacent to where they spent the summer. If no true estuary is nearby, they will often seek the deeper holes and channels in bays. When the water temperature falls into the fifties, there will be a distinct movement of mature males out of shallow water. An early northwester and the passage of a cold front can make Jimmies disappear almost overnight and so can an early snow squall. If and when the water temperature falls to about 40°F. crabs will bury themselves almost completely in the mud, there to lie semi-dormant until spring.

When the new season once again hearkens, males basically climb back up into shallow water, though a great many will die during or just after their second winter. The females that awaken may nose a bit closer to the ocean, to salinities approaching pure seawater, as their young will need these salty waters to survive. After dropping their eggs, their life cycle is completed, and most will die. Crabs hatched in late summer will often make it through a third summer and even a third winter. But few will see a fourth summer.

FEEDING HABITS AND BAITS. The blue claw crab eats both plant and animal matter, living and dead. Many perceive this crab to be a scavenger, and in fact he will mop up almost any type of dead meat or fish he happens upon. Yet most experienced crabbers agree that fresh fish is the bait that usually works best. Fish that is quickly frozen then thawed is perfectly fine, a few say even better.

Professional potters usually prefer herring when it is available. These are oily fish, and that is not by accident. Almost all of the preferred baits are oily. Besides the two spring herring—alewife and blueback herring—bluefish, eel, menhaden (mossbunker) and butterfish are all oily and make good bait. Perhaps oily fish smell stronger or otherwise attract crabs better. It's a point to remember.

Special strong, long-handled tongs are made for the crabber, and they really make culling much easier and safer. Look for them in sport shops near popular crabbing grounds.

Experiment with different baits. Rudy Peknic, of Bayside, NY, likes whole fish carcasses that have been fileted. Small pieces of meat, he thinks, drift off as the day wears on, possibly acting like a chum screen. I personally have had very good luck with flounder heads, whiting heads, and whole snapper blues. Fish heads, especially small bluefish heads, work better for me than chunks of fish, and they last much longer. Oddly, mackerel is one oily fish that I have had poor luck with. Baits that occur naturally where you are crabbing may be a plus.

TIDES, TIME OF DAY, AND WEATHER. Crabs are very unpredictable, and there are exceptions to every crabbing rule. But we almost always prefer the first half of the rising tide at the crack of dawn. This is especially true on bright days or on big, shadeless waters. Herein, I firmly believe, lies the reason why most crabbers fail to fill the bushel: They simply arrive too late.

Add a little cloud cover, a light-refracting chop, or a little turbidity though, and you are liable to have better mid-day sport. If you have to crab between 11 a.m. and dark, at least try to hit the rising tide.

The effects and mechanics of tides and currents are enormously varied, and there are many places where a rising tide is the wrong tide. One example might be where the tide is "squeezed" through a narrow bridge, strait, channel or other "funnel." The crab may not be able to linger long enough to sample your bait. Search for the quieter waters behind these funnels. Or try the slow half of the falling tide. Overall, you will just have to learn the waters where you crab, since each place is different. But you can be pretty sure that 4 to 10 a.m. will be the best time.

If you're counting on catching your crab bait, don't go at dead low tide. It's usually the worst time. Half up to high is often good.

I've gone out on rainy days and caught absolutely zilch. Most crabbers agree that rainy days are not as good, though I have heard of some impressive exceptions. The passage of a strong cold front affects all shallow-water marine animals, often suppressing their activity and driving them deeper. Better crabbing may be associated with the improving weather two days after the passage of a cold front.

Most sport crabbing is done in waters 5 to 15 feet deep.

TWO

Finding Crabs

It is not difficult to learn the various crabbing methods. Nor is it hard to catch the blue claw once you find him. Compared to the whitetailed deer, for example, or the brown trout, he is easily tricked. The real challenge—if you desire to catch of lot of crabs, more of the time—is finding crab concentrations.

AN OVERVIEW OF CRAB HABITAT. The foremost thing to remember is this: The blue claw is a denizen of neither the open ocean nor pure, fresh water, but places where the two waters mix. Other sections in this book describe the importance of *correct* salinities at various stages of the blue claw's life. This chapter takes that all-important salinity factor, and other factors, and attempts to translate them to help you find the most crabs. It also suggests which methods to use in which locations.

To have the gradient of salinities needed for a blue claw to complete its life cycle, you must have an infusion of fresh water. Therefore, as simple as it sounds, the first thing to seek out is a place where a river meets the ocean. Whether you crab from bridge or pier, in bays or tidal rivers, or along the inland waterways—all discussed in detail later in this chapter—you must have fresh water

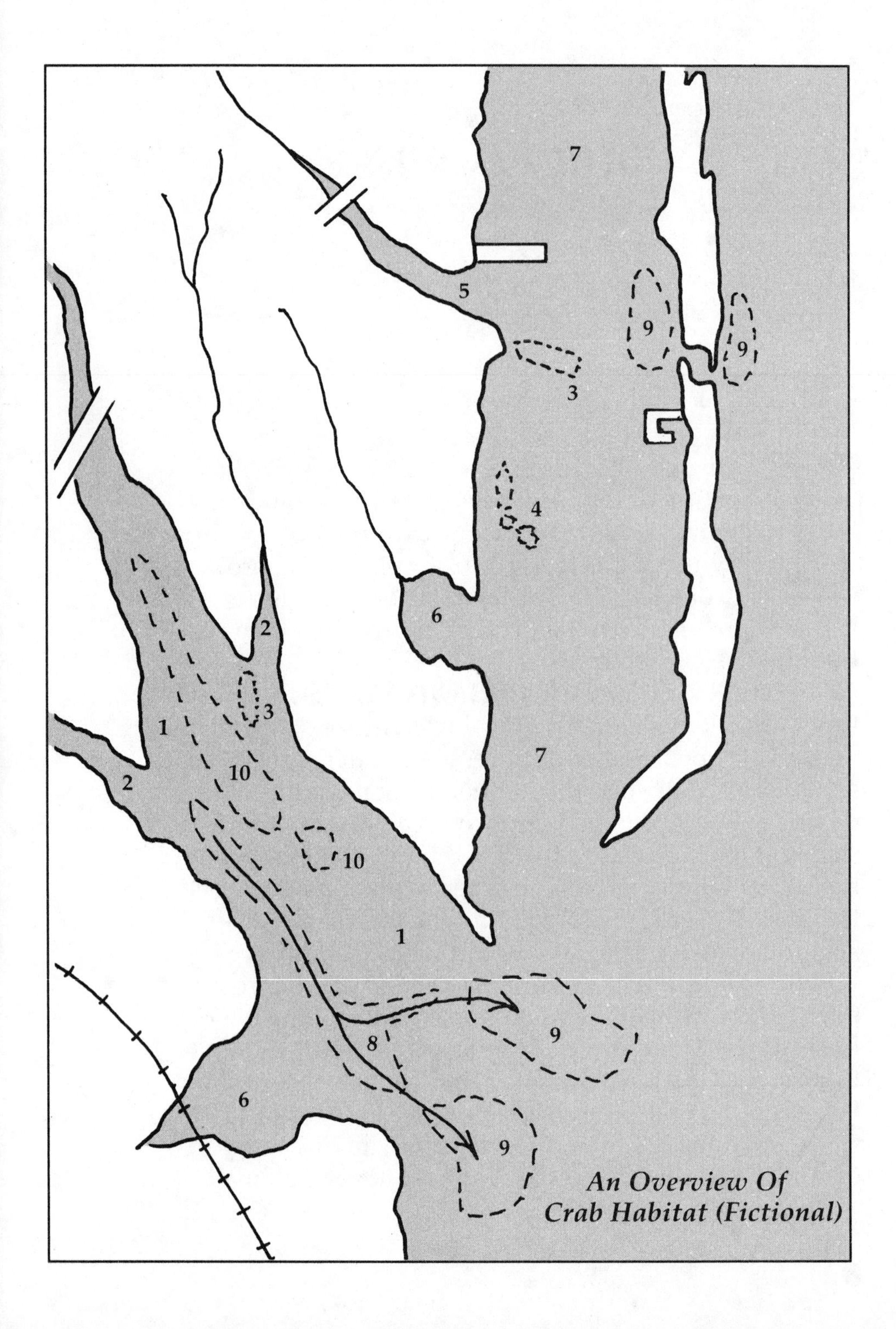

An Overview Of Crab Habitat (Fictional)

coming from somewhere. The best kind of river, and the best place to crab, is not a true river at all but an estuary (p. 10, #1).

Typified by Chesapeake Bay, the most productive crabbing ground in the world, an estuary is an arm of the sea that is protected but still open enough to allow a strong influx of salt water. There must also be strong infusions from a fresh water river, or in the case of the Chesapeake, rivers. A "good" estuary, in terms of crab production, should have plenty of shallow water, and subsequently, healthy marshlands and much rooted, aquatic vegetation. Yet there should also be some deeper holes or river channels. Such an estuary will provide the greatest acreage of suitable crab habitat, and also the greatest production per acre.

Just as important, these big estuaries always have contributory waters (#2). To the sport crabber who lacks the fair-sized boat and equipment needed to crab on big waters, these tributaries can be ideal: providing easy access *plus* proximity to the rich nursery grounds of the main estuary. To put it another way, I'd rather crab in a tidal river that feeds into a fertile estuary than one that simply flows into the ocean.

In spite of everything else I tell you, remember that the crab is a roamer. Foot loose and fancy free crabbers will gather in more of this delectable shellfish. At no time is this more true than in summer, when nearly the entire shallow water area of an estuary may produce. By shallow, I mean depths of 20 feet or less. Sometimes, natural or unnatural bottom features will hold crabs. Included here are shoals and bars created by rivers (#3), submerged beds of dense weeds, deeper holes, human refuse (#4), and so forth. These are some of the places to seek out if you find yourself crabbing on wide-open spaces.

An estuary, though, isn't the only place to look for

crabs. There are for example no estuaries on Long Island, yet there are blue claws. If you do not live near a true estuary, here are some other places where the fresh and salt water mix may be favorable.

As already mentioned, tidal rivers to hold crabs do not have to feed into a large, estuarine system. These can flow directly into the ocean (#5). Bays, really indentations in the shoreline as used in this book, can "trap" fresh water run-off and be very crabby (#6). The entire intercoastal waterway (#7) acts as a block to the sea, trapping enough fresh water to create brackish conditions and, often, excellent crabbing. Before we discuss these important features in detail, though, let's first look at a question that most crabbers find of interest.

HOW TO EXTEND YOUR CRABBING SEASON. Where do the crabs go? How can you jump the gun and catch them in April or May? Can crabs still be caught from late October to early December, or even in winter? Almost all sport crabbers have wondered these things at one time or another, and few among the fraternity would not like to know how to catch crabs outside the traditional summer season. The section titled "Life Cycle" in Ch. 1 provides some of the answers. Here is a look at some specific strategies to extend your crabbing season.

First, we must know our limitations. From New Jersey to Virginia, crabs are usually buried in the mud and unavailable except to commercial dredgers from approximately December through February. From New York northward, the dormancy might extend from late November through part of April. In the Carolinas, winter dormancy is shorter, and south of that, it is shorter still. In the tepid waters off Florida and the Gulf states, crabs can be caught at all times of year, though their activity may slow down in January and February.

From the central Atlantic northward, though, October

and November is a time of movement. After mating, females will quickly head down bay or estuary, and they can be intercepted or even followed if you can find the migratory route (#8). It is generally thought that they stay in quite shallow water, perhaps following shoals and even man-made canals and waterways. Most fertilized females winter near estuary mouths or other salty waters (#9), but if they arrive a little early, they will still be somewhat active. Find these wintering grounds and you may catch them in late October or November before they burrow.

Mature, keeping-size males slowly move off into deeper channels and holes. If the weather holds up, they may stay in the shallows right through October and even November. In November, you can start trying progressively deeper water. A harsh, autumnal storm may quickly push them out though, so if they seem to disappear following an early blow, try much deeper. In late November and December (again, in the central Atlantic region), they will likely be very deep—30-60 feet or more (#10)—but they still may be catchable in pots and traps until the water temperature at their depth hits 40°F. This temperature will bring on almost immediate burrowing.

In spring, females bred the previous fall (the ones that migrated) will still be near the ocean (#9). Come late March and early April, they will start to wiggle around again and may feed quite actively. If you find them, you may be able to catch them. Females not bred the previous fall, either because they hatched late or just did not find a mate, may not have even migrated seaward. In late May or June, they will be anxious to breed, and may be taken by "Jimmy potting" (see Ch. 3).

Both one and two-year-old males that survived the winter start climbing back up into the shallows. In April, you can try pots or traps in the same deeper holes and

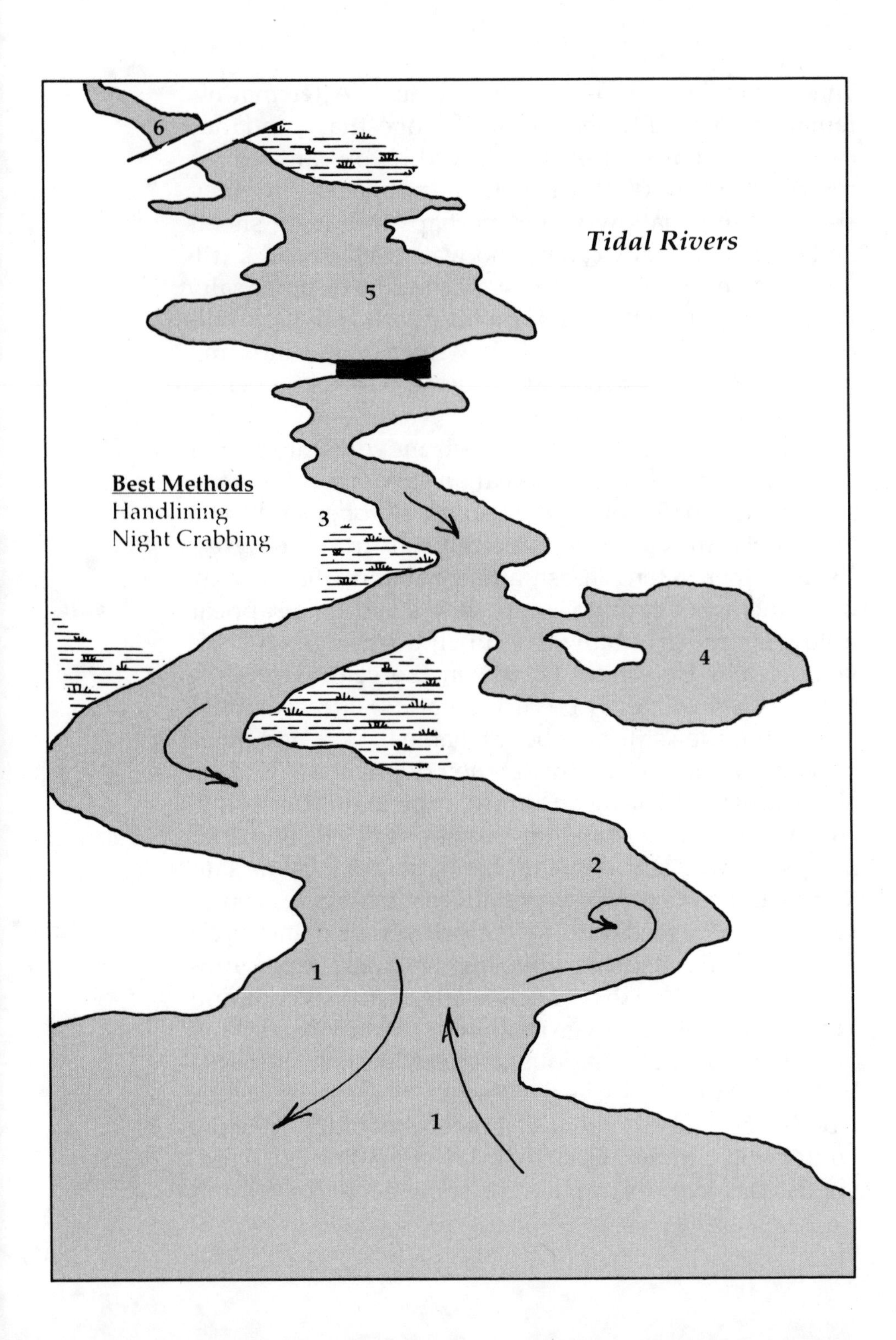
Tidal Rivers
Best Methods
Handlining
Night Crabbing
6
5
3
4
2
1
1

channels near the middle of river or estuary or in some cases, bay or sound. Through May and early June, try progressively shallower water, concentrating especially on contour breaks.

TIDAL RIVERS. These set the stage for some of the finest crabbing. They might also be called sub-estuaries, being, in fact, estuaries in miniature. But some will empty into a sound, a strait, or even directly into the ocean . . . not into a bigger estuarine system. What we're really talking about here are streams averaging 15 to 50 feet wide. There are two types.

The first is not a true tidal river, but really just an arm of the sea. It is a natural or man-created channel that fills up at high tide, but does not have a fresh water stream feeding it. Thus at low tide, it may be stagnant or even completely dry. Such a "river" might better be called a marsh, simply receiving and discharging the sea. Crabbing-wise, it will not usually be too productive.

A true tidal river is always "running," because it is fed by fresh water. Even though it may shrink to a tiny, mud-surrounded channel at dead low tide, there will still be some flow.

Crabs love these tidal rivers and it will pay you to find a good one. As in so many types of fishing and hunting, maps are invaluable. Start by examining some of the bigger estuaries. Does the map reveal smaller streams feeding in? It doesn't take a very big one to support blue claws and, in fact, many small tidal rivers are completely overlooked. I know one a scant mile from my home running into the Hudson River. I don't think anyone else crabs it but me. If your state or county map doesn't show enough detail, get a hold of some town maps, often available from the Chamber of Commerce.

Moreso than some of the bigger waters, tides can be very significant when crabbing tidal rivers. There is no question that crabs sweep in with a rising tide, and I've found the most concentrated action then. However, there is another factor here, one that few people seem to be aware of: elevation. Some rivers will not get a full, 6-hour tide because they are too far above sea level; only the last few hours of the rising tide may reach a certain section of a tidal river. One such river in Connecticut used to have us perplexed until we figured this out. The tide would come in for two hours only, and to catch any amount of crabs you had to be there at that time. Then the tide would go out for 10 hours. Of course, what's happening is this: two hours up tide, two hours down tide, eight hours fresh water river flowing by. The moral is that tide tables aren't enough. You just have to figure out the tides on your own river. As an aside, it's interesting to note that we still caught *some* crabs during the fresh water river phase. Mature crabs can move freely between fresh and salt water. "Osmo-regulator" is the fancy term scientists use to describe an organism that can do this.

If the river feeds directly into the ocean (p. 14, #1), you may have to go quite far upstream to find crabs. However, if the river feeds into another brackish water, like a sound or a larger estuary, the mouth of the tidal river could be a superb place to try. Depending upon the strength of the tide, the main channel may be good, but the backwashes may be even better (#2). Always look for quiet waters in the lee of faster waters. River mouths, by the way, can be excellent places to scap crabs at night.

On the inside bends of a tidal river (#3), you can occasionally get lucky and find a few peelers—crabs ready to moult into softshells. What happens is that some peelers simply do not hide themselves well enough when their time to shed approaches. Thus at dead low tide, they may be visible. A few times, I have seen the shape of a crab just barely discernible in the mud. These have sometimes turned out to be softshells, slightly buried in the mud or just well camouflaged along the bank.

Walk the river and look for oxbows, or quiet little "ponds" (#4). My theory is that in early and mid-summer, fewer crabs go out with the tide than come in with it. They may use these sidewaters for resting and mating. Later in the season, the situation may reverse, with more crabs going out than coming in.

Continue walking upstream. If it's too marshy, a small boat or canoe can take explorers into waters never seen by others. If you can find a pond or pool just above the tide line (#5), you may have found a bonanza. The pond may be somehow isolated, say by a small dam or just by elevation. But if it is within reach of an unusually big tide, crabs may be swept in and then trapped. We know of one such pond in Connecticut where we catch near lobster-size blue claws side by side with barefoot boys floating bobbers for sunfish and perch! Yet this pond only produces at the crack of dawn. Here, then, is another theory: The more still and clear the waters, the more important it is to arrive early in the morning.

Finally, don't be afraid to venture way upstream, even past where the highest tide goes (#6). Especially during the late summer breeding period, crabs may go way inland. Try these places at night.

BAYS. A bay is used to describe many types of water, both fresh and salt. For now, let us think of it as an

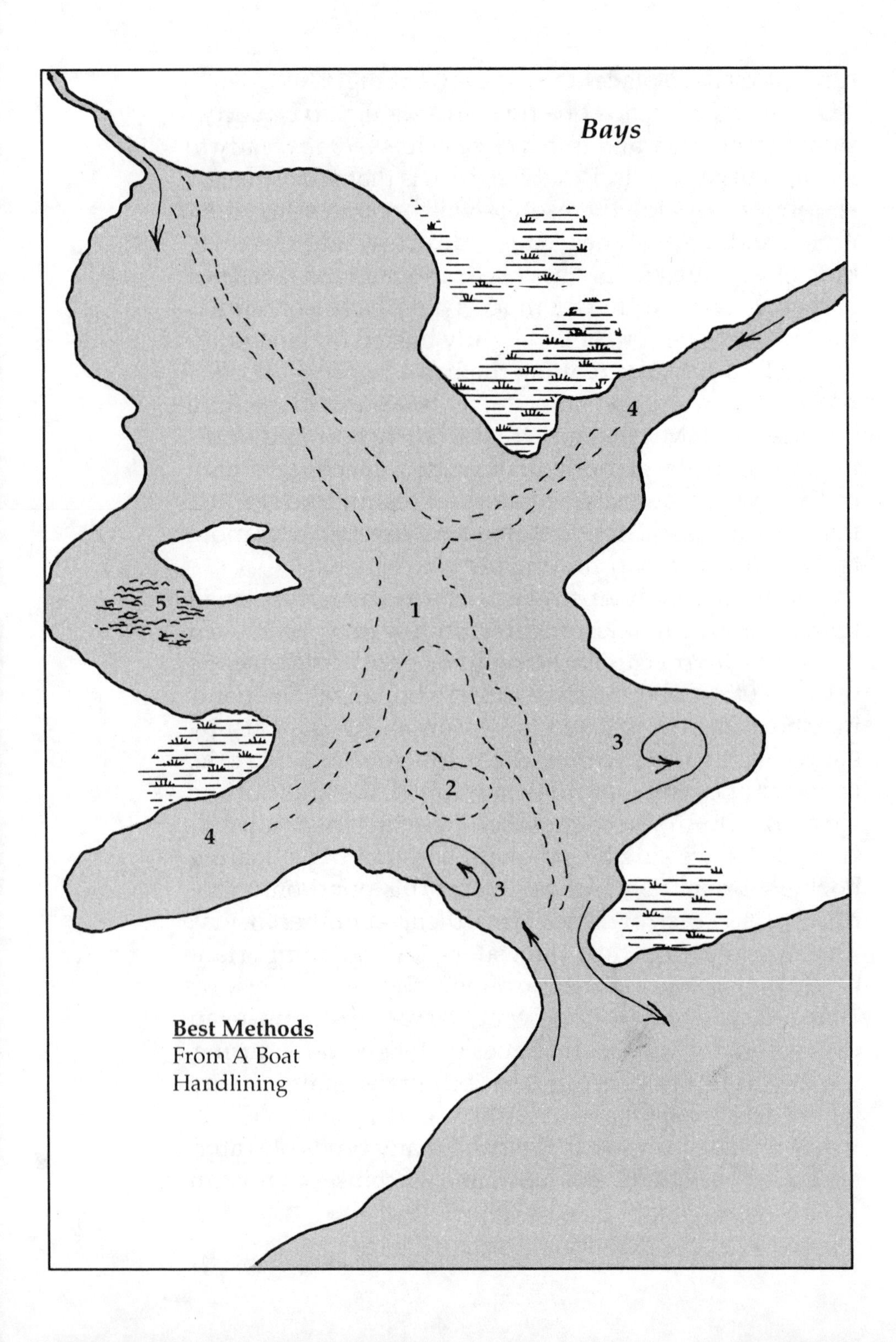
Bays
1
2
3
3
4
4
5
Best Methods
From A Boat
Handlining

indentation in the shoreline, more sheltered and generally shallower than the ocean, and *not having* an especially strong influx of fresh water. It will be useful for discussing certain aspects of crabs and crabbing, though these may also apply to some of the other habitat types mentioned in this chapter.

If it is directly adjacent to the ocean and has no stream feeding it, it may be pure seawater. In most instances, such a bay won't be too crabby. The best bays are within estuaries, or adjacent to inland waterways or bigger tidal rivers. Again, we are usually looking for the middle salinities, 10-24 ppt., to find the best crabbing.

Some bays are very shallow; this is good for crabs . . . up to a point. But if the water is a scant few feet, crabs may move strictly within the channels. Even in the absence of tributaries, there may be an old stream channel (p. 18, #1) or channels, and these can be found by probing with an oar or a long stick. Sometimes an extra low tide will reveal the deeper spots, and you can also watch the tides. Generally, the tide will move more quickly over deep water than over shallow. If you find a deep hole (#2), you may hit paydirt. Often the crabs will group up in these holes, especially when the sun is bright.

Not just in bays, but anywhere, watch for contrasting currents: slow next to fast. In the frothy backwaters inside faster currents (#3) crabs will often concentrate, perhaps looking for food. These backwaters are often within reach of boatless crabbers tossing cages or handlines from shore. Additionally, contrasting currents or "rips" frequently belie the presence of sand bars, which can also hold crabs.

If there are any side arms or channels running off the main bay (#4), don't fail to give them a try. There are two such arms in a bay we crab, and they are generally dead for the first two hours of the rising tide. At that time the mouth of the bay produces better. Then the action at the mouth stops, and when the tide is two hours up, we string our traps around these side channels . . . and often double our morning's catch. Logically, crabs should move further into a bay as the tide rises. But to repeat: Try different locations at different stages of the tide.

The best way to learn little tricks of the trade is to watch old timers. Very seldom will these salty, grizzled, and usually clam-mouthed pros venture much information. But that doesn't mean you can't spy on them. I caught one old timer—he always had a full bushel—cutting his fresh fish lengthwise, and turning it completely inside out before tying it into the trap with a string. This bloody bow-tie must look like eggs benedict to the crabs! And it does work better than a half frozen lump of meat. It might always be a good idea to open a fish somewhat, especially when using firm, mild smelling fish. To attract crabs in very murky water, some people hang the bait down from the top of the trap.

Being somewhat quieter than fast-moving tidal rivers, and often too shallow for noisy powerboaters, bay-like waters may be where a lot of peelers go to shed. If you can find a submerged bed of thick, rooted vegetation (#5)—eelgrass being the best—you have a potential crab bonanza at your fingertips.

There are a couple of other conditions that can attract crabs by the droves. Both are unnatural, and neither have to be associated with bays. You might find them anywhere along the coast. One is the warm water effluent from a power plant. Certain fish can be caught year-round in these man made bathtubs and so can crabs. Another one is around a garbage dump. Food garbage draws crabs like a magnet. Strict laws now prevent such dumping, but any waters adjacent to an existing dump could be a gold mine of blue claws.

BRIDGES. There are thousands and thousands of bridges along the Atlantic Coast, and from them, some of the best crabbing is to be had. These run the gamut from single-lane wooden spans over tidal rivers, to railroad trestles to intercoastal bridges many miles long. There are several reasons why bridges help provide so much good sport for crabbers.

First, most people don't have boats, so a bridge can give you a little mobility. You can try close to shore, or out in the middle, or anywhere in between. And you can crab with a bare minimum of gear. Second, there is very little fouling of traps, since they land squarely with all four doors opening most of the time (toss them from shore and it's hit or miss). You can also see where the action is; the more crabbers, the better the action. Finally, bridges may provide the only safe footing in the often marshy environment the blue claw calls home.

As mentioned previously, maps can help you find tidal rivers and they can also help you pinpoint the bridges that cross them. Whenever I drive across a

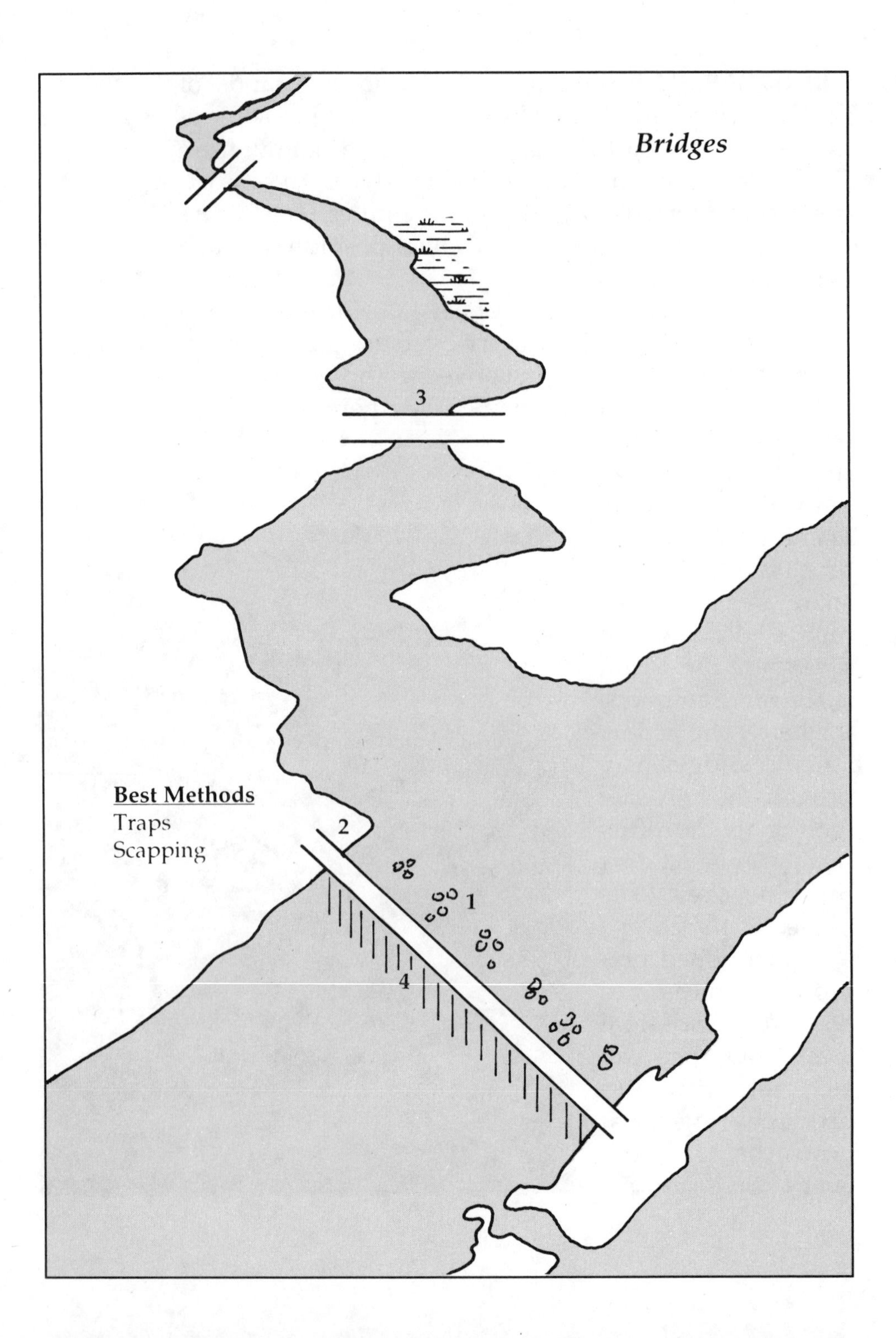
Bridges
3
Best Methods
Traps
Scapping
2
1
4

tidal river, I look for telltale pieces of string, or scraps of weeds or fish that can give away a hot bridge. We normally set traps off the bridge, though sometimes we also work handlines along the banks of the waterway the bridge crosses.

In many instances, rows of old pilings can be found adjacent to newer bridges (p. 22, #1). These pilings were footings for older bridges now long gone. An adroit scap netter can have a field day just going from one piling to another, though he may also have to set some traps to fill out a bushel.

If crabbing is prohibited from the bridge as, alas, it often is, try the corner abutments (#2). Seldom will anyone bother you here. Bridge abutments are one of the things crabs love to latch onto, so don't fail to bring a long handled scap net anytime you crab from or around a bridge. If the bridge happens to span a narrow waterway between two larger bodies of water (#3), it might be an excellent place to scap crabs. I believe that the very fast currents associated with such funnels cause crabs to ride in along the top. I have seen it so many times.

While bridge crabbing is just like most other types of crabbing, best in early morning, this type of structure can cast shadows on the water. When the sun gets high, you can extend your day just by working waters in the shade of larger bridges (#4).

PIERS, DOCKS AND BULKHEADS. These structures are good for crabbing for many of the same reasons as are bridges. Once again, we want to look for them where they project out into brackish waters, not directly into the ocean. You *might* take a few blue claws off the Steel Pier in Atlantic City. But I think your odds would be better at one of the gambling casinos.

Fishing piers (p.24, #1) are often fine places to crab. If fishing is permitted, so will crabbing be. Some piers are

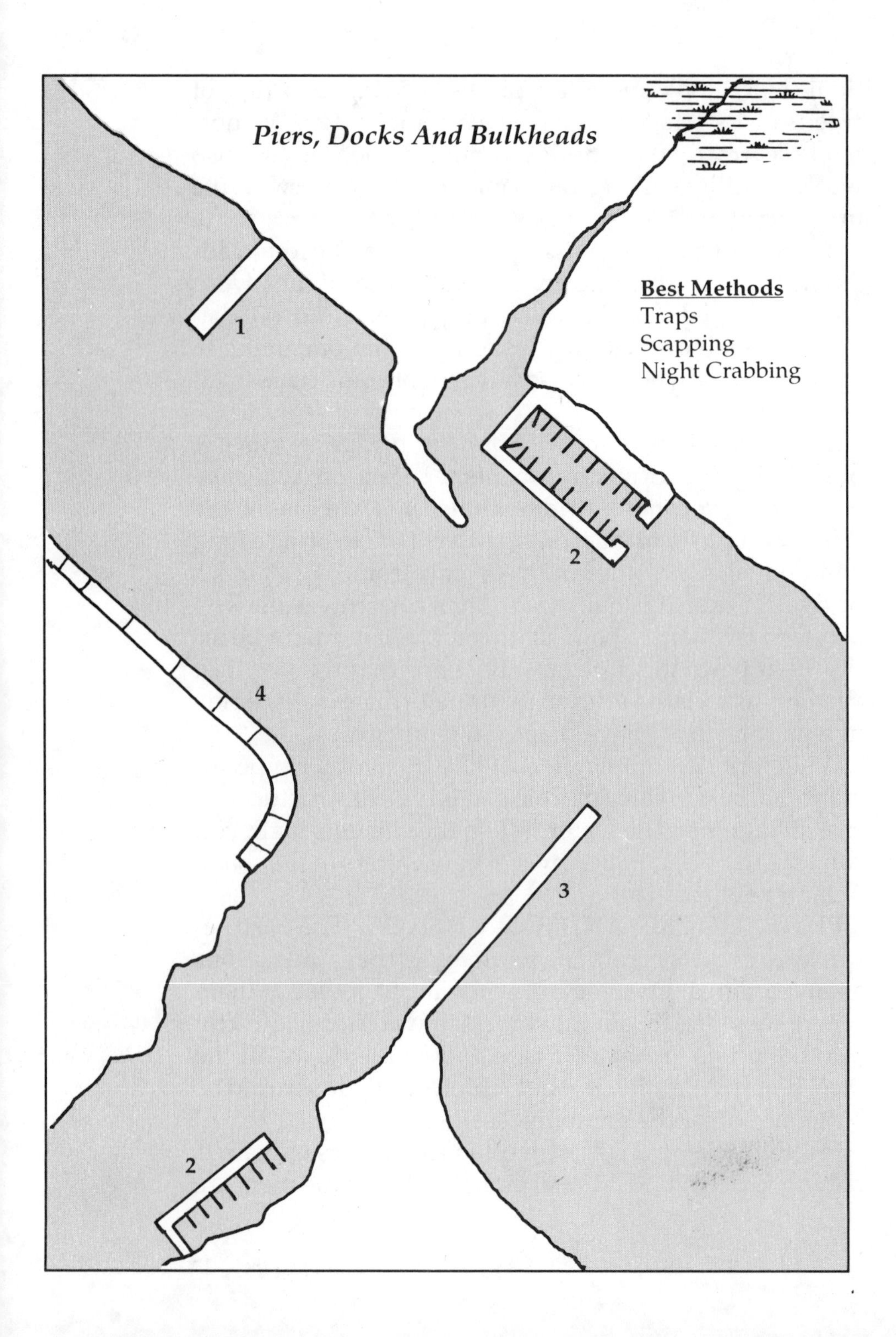

Piers, Docks And Bulkheads
Best Methods
Traps
Scapping
Night Crabbing
1
2
4
3
2

quite long, and can thus get you out over a variety of waters. There may be a modest fee, typically $.50 or $1.00, to get out on the pier. A bait concession may be present.

Private or public docks (#2) are good places to toss traps. Along the lower Hudson where I live, access to the water (where there are no interfering rocks) is very limited. Happily, some marinas do grant permission to crabbers, though you often have to be a member or know one. A few expert crabbers of my acquaintance crab day after day off a certain marina. "To keep the crabs around," they say, they chum the area with scraps of meat and fish. The whole idea of chumming for crabs is an interesting one, worth exploring.

Crabbing from marinas is always a strong bet. Here, Tarrytown, New York's famous Tappan Zee Bridge is in the background.

Docks and piers will not only get you out over the water, they will often attract crabs. First, there may be some lights overhead, which will draw crabs at night. This can make for some dandy, midnight scapping. Crabs will also come to hang onto the pilings, for whatever reasons

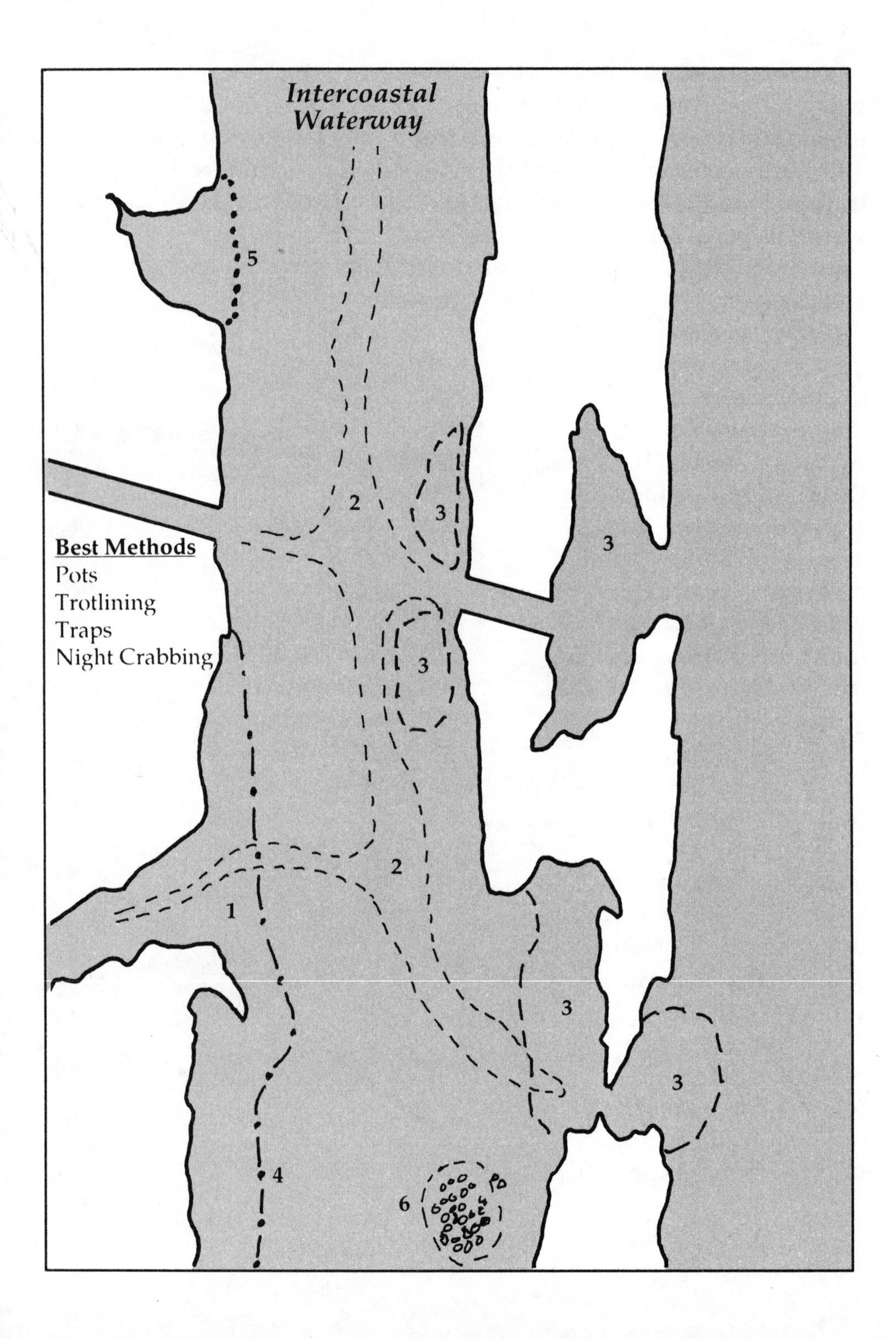

Intercoastal Waterway
5
2
3
3
3
Best Methods
Pots
Trotlining
Traps
Night Crabbing
2
1
3
3
4
6

they are wont to do so. In the daytime they'll come for the shade, too, and for the old bait and cleaned fish that may be discarded by anglers.

Breakwaters (#3), also called jetties, can sometimes be excellent crabbing platforms. Many of these structures are built adjacent to parks or beaches, to promote better conditions for bathing or boating, or to protect a harbor. Look for them especially at the mouths of tidal rivers. Work traps or handlines in the slower water inside the current, but bring along a scap net, too.

Bulkheads and retaining walls (#4) provide yet another place to crab, and unlike many marinas, are often open to the public. Box traps are the best devices for crabbing off of these man-made structures.

INTERCOASTAL WATERWAY. We can thank both man and nature for providing excellent crabbing grounds in the form of the intercoastal waterway. This safe, inshore passageway was begun by the barrier islands, and man added his touches in the form of canals, dug channels, retaining walls, bridges, and so on. Crabs may be found anywhere, but crabbing in these waterways will be best near where fresh water rivers enter (p. 26, #1). An excellent example is Tom's River, located on New Jersey's Barnegat Bay.

Very often, there will be old river channels (#2) and these may be where the crabs go in winter. This is the way it is in estuaries, and there's every reason to believe that blue claws follow this pattern in the inshore waterways. Of course in winter they will be dormant, but at either end of winter, you should try these deeper waters (see "extending your crabbing season" earlier in this chapter). Standard marine charts will give you accurate depths; you can also find the channels by watching where the larger ships go. If you run pots, stay on the fringes of the channels, so you don't get your lines cut by propellers.

While the males and immature females may seek these deeper channels during cold weather, the fertilized females will move to shallower, saltier water in autumn. Some places to hunt for females, in late autumn and early spring, would be on both sides of inlets or canals (#3) or in some lagoons and bays where salinities are very high (almost pure seawater).

Coastal bait & tackle shops are your best source of local crabbing info.

In spring and early summer, action seems to pick up quickly, and the intercoastal waterways get hot before many inland rivers and estuaries. Try them early in the season. Trotlining is a popular method on these big waters, and there are several approaches you can take. The first break to deeper water (#4) can be a good starting point. If you can locate such a break, lay your trotline along it and parallel to shore. Some trotliners also set their lines across the mouth of the bay (#5), hoping to catch crabs moving from shallow water to deeper water. Such a lay can be quite productive in early morning. Many crabbers swear that old oyster or other shellfish beds are top places to set pots or traps (#6); try over the many types of bottom structure described throughout this chapter.

Crabs usually prefer a fairly clean sandy or muddy bottom. However, bottom "structure" may attract them at times.

THREE
Methods of Capture & Gear

We'll call them traps here, but they're also known as nets, baskets and cages. There are four or five types used by sport crabbers, and all operate on the same simple principle. The trap is baited and lowered to the bottom, and the crabber then waits a prescribed period of time. When he hoists the rope attached to the trap, the victim is captured.

The ring net is simplest and least expensive. Essentially, this contrivance consists of two metal hoops of different sizes connected by cotton or synthetic netting. A piece of bait is tied into the wire mesh within the *inner* hoop, and when the trap is hoisted, the *outer* hoop, which is larger, pulls up and traps the crab(s).

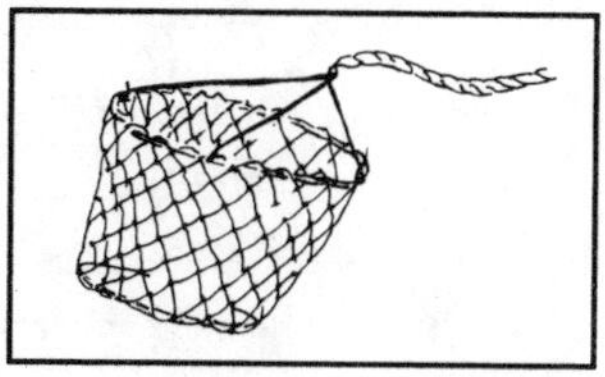

The device has many shortcomings. First, the bottom must be fairly clean and level. Rocks or rubble will render ring nets pretty much unusable. Neither can this trap be flung around as much as a box trap; best to lower it straight down. Nonetheless, the ring net is an OK method for young crabbers on a paper route budget.

Gaining popularity is the low-profile trap. This is just a

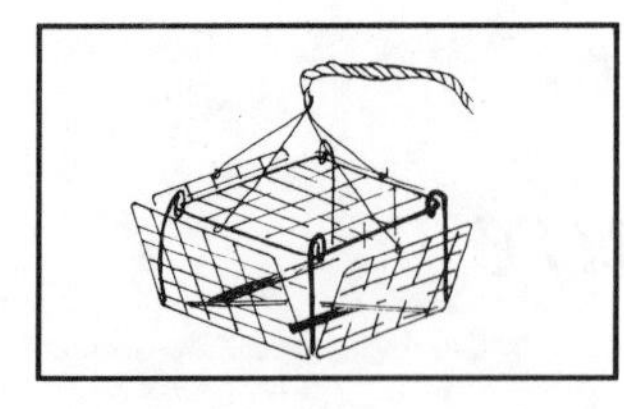

The low profile box trap (top) has gained widespread acceptance among crabbers. It offers several advantages and few disadvantages. Nonetheless, the standard box trap (below) remains the more popular style.

cut down version of the standard box trap, and its design makes a world of sense. Who needs all that metal? Being only about six inches high, the minis take up less space. You can thus transport and deploy more of them. The doors also close more quickly. This definitely lessens the incidence of crabs escaping when you tighten up on the rope. The minis also present less resistance to the current, so they're less likely to be bowled over.

Still, the standard box trap remains the primary nemesis of *Callinectes* in many areas, especially from New Jersey northward. All of the following tips about rigging and fishing box traps also apply to the minis.

When buying box traps, stick with the standard models. The gauge of the wire mesh varies considerably. Wire that is unusually thick or spaced unusually close together seems to catch fewer crabs. When assembling, you'll note that your "kit" gives you very fine line to rig the doors. This delicate little string is worthless. Replace it with something stouter, preferably a strong, slick-surfaced cotton. For the running line, we've found that a floating material—we use 3/8 inch Polypropylene—has at least four advantages. One: If you're crabbing from a boat, the floating line will let you see how the tide is moving. Two: It makes pulling easier and smoother. Three: If your buoy comes untied, you won't lose your trap. Four: If you're tossing your cages from shore, the floating line will be far less likely to snag among shoreline rocks and debris.

When you rig the doors of the trap, one piece of cord per door, leave a little excess to allow for shrinkage. If the string is too short, the door will not open all the way, and if it is too long, it will keep the doors from closing fully.

If there was just one thing I could tell you about traps, it would be this: In most places, especially those with strong currents, traps just don't open properly. If you can eliminate this problem, you will double your take of crabs. A simple way to fight the tide is with heavy bank or pyramid sinkers. These can be tied to the bottom of the frame. But there is a much better way. Obtain some lengths of concrete reinforcing rod. Cut these to match in length the side of a trap, and wire two onto the inside bottom of the trap on facing sides. This will anchor the center. If you still have problems with the doors not opening, a much lighter steel rod can be wired onto the outside edges of each door.

The easiest way to bait a trap is with wire. You can simply leave it in there trip after trip. Like many crabbers, though, I'm fussy. I prefer string for no reason I can communicate. Fish heads are probably best. Tie one in through the eye socket and it will be in that trap all day (unless a big old snappin' turtle comes calling!) It's amazing, too, how crabs will keep coming in for a fish head even when there no longer seems to be a scrap of anything worth eating on it.

America's tinkerers and entrepreneurs are constantly coming up with new crab trap designs. At top is the "Crab Napper", the most compact crab trap I've yet seen. Below that is a vinyl-coated 2-door trap. Note bent doors (for tighter closure) and bait box in center.

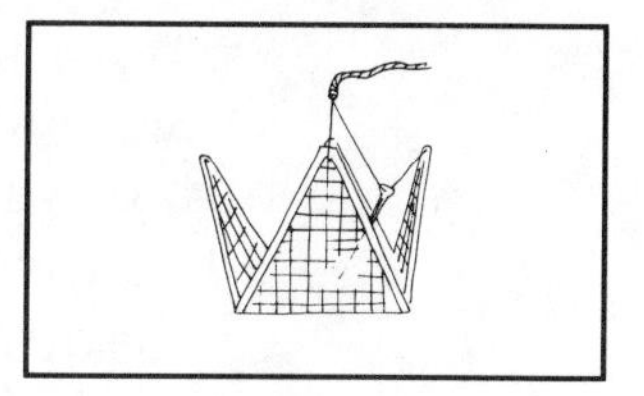

Star or "Pyramid" crab trap.

One more well entrenched trap is the pyramid or star trap. Its chief advantage is that it folds flat for much easier storage and transportation. This device never seems to work as smoothly as the box trap, so we seldom use it.

Though it may not seem so, how long you wait between pulls can be extremely important. When the crabs are moving, you should check your traps almost continuously. In many locations, we've gotten 75% of our day's take within an hour. Frequently, this has been from a half hour after the start of the rising tide and for one hour thereafter. Very often it's also been the first hour of daylight, regardless of the tide.

HANDLINES. There is no more fun or challenging way to catch crabs than with a handline. This takes skill and dexterity, a sharp eye, and a fast hand. It's a perfect way to get the entire family involved. You can work in teams and switch off seeing who works best with whom. Or, you can operate your handlines alone, which is even tougher.

For the beginner, here's how it goes. You fasten a piece of bait to a long string, toss it into waters where crabs are known to be, and wait for one (or occasionally two) to pick up the bait. You can always tell. They'll be a tugging on the line, and it may even be moving from side to side. Then the line is pulled in slowly, and the operator, or his partner, scaps the crab as soon as it comes into sight.

Blue crabs have keen senses, and it's important to use stealth when approaching bank or shore. If the water is very clear, you must be even quieter. However, under these conditions crabs will drop off sooner, so somewhat turbid waters make for better handlining.

There is suspense and excitement in this! The line itself can be any old piece of string, not too thick. As to length, this will depend on where you are crabbing, but 20 feet is usually enough. For the occasions where you are working alone, a 6-foot scap net is the ticket. A longer one would be too cumbersome to handle in addition to the line. Even when you work in teams, the net will seldom need be more than six feet. Wooden handles, shallow netting, and a 10-inch hoop typify this type of scap net.

Your handline's terminal rig must hold the bait *and* provide enough weight to keep the bait on bottom. There are several options, some of which are depicted in the accompanying drawings.

Fish heads again are tough to beat. With a knife, poke the end of the line in one eye socket and out the other, but slip on a sinker before tying off. The strength of the current will tell you how heavy a sinker to use, but one to three ounces is generally good. Another fine rig is a "killy ring." This is simply a circle of fresh-caught killifish or other small baitfish strung on a hoop of flexible wire. The wire provides what is often enough weight, and possibly, gives the crab something to hold onto. It's a good outfit. Creative crabbers have also fashioned terminal

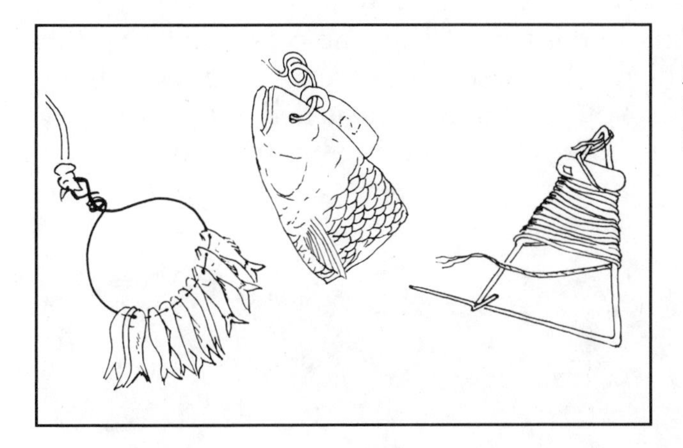

Three popular terminal rigs for handlines (l to r): killy ring, fish head and "safety pin".

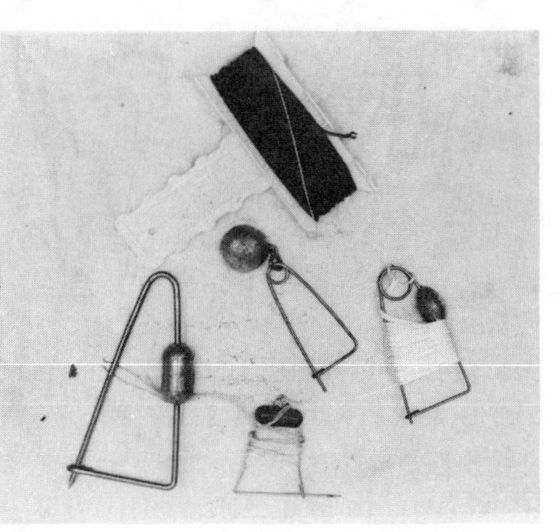

Four types of commercially made terminal rigs for handlines, all operating on the safety pin concept. At top is a standard dropline used by fishermen. It can be used by crabbers, too.

rigs out of electrical clamps (weight *plus* a good means of holding soft bait if that's all you have), old padlocks, eyebolts, and almost anything else with a loop on it. There are also commercially made handline rigs.

There are at least four ways to work a handline. It can be fished from a boat. It can be tied to a dock or pier. It can be worked from the banks. Or it can be tied to a stake and fished *in* the water. Photos within the chapter illustrate some of these methods.

Within his watery domain, the crab will be more likely to hold on. That's why handlining from a boat works well. Even better may be handlining while you're actually standing in the water. The crab comes in along the bottom, which is less likely to scare him than a straight vertical pull. Your end of the line is tied to a stake 10 or 15 feet from shore. Then, wearing hip boots or bathing suit, or just with rolled up trousers, you go to it. Of course

wherever you run a handline, you won't want to run just one. Serious crabbers use three, four or more, so they are almost constantly busy.

It's remarkable to the novice crabber that the crab will hold on. He will! But only if you retrieve the line slowly and smoothly. Further, he'll only hang on for so long. Four feet from shore or a half foot from the surface is the usual breaking point. That's why the scap man should place his net on bottom, just offshore at arm's reach, while the line operator maneuvers the crab over the net. The netter has to be fast, pulling at just the right moment. Frustration and arguments generally follow a missed crab, which occurs none too infrequently.

SCAPPING. A scap net is used in conjunction with handlining and night crabbing, covered elsewhere in this chapter, but here we will talk about daytime scapping when nothing more than the scap net is used.

The first time you try to scap a crab, you'll learn at least three things about him: He has excellent eyesight (almost 360°!), he's fast, and he can swim sideways. All these factors must be considered when you're skulking along an old dock or pier looking for an easy meal. Like handlining, scapping takes good reflexes. In essence, it means locating a moving or stationary crab (in places described throughout Ch. 2) and then simply "scapping him up." The 6-foot wood-handled net recommended for handlining is not adequate here. You can try making a 6-foot extension for your wooden net, but you'd be better advised to buy the 10 or 12-foot aluminum scap nets made for crabbing. In these lengths, wood would be too heavy. In certain locales, notably off bridges, I have seen home-fashioned scap nets that looked to be all of 16 feet. This raises the question of transportability. The biggest homemade scap nets I've seen could be broken down into pieces. Even an eight foot net will pose a problem if you happen to own a small car. Then you might *have to* make your own. Commercially made telescoping scap nets are available but you might have to do some hunting to find one.

Fourteen inches seems like a good diameter for the

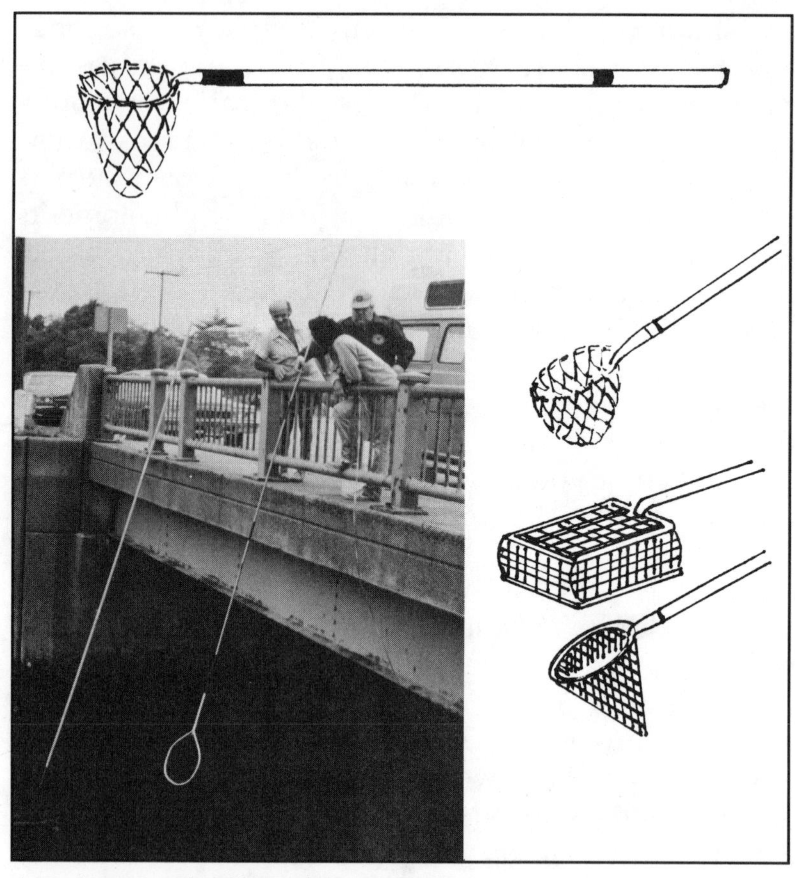

A good scap net should be at least 10 feet long, though much longer ones are often needed (photo). At the right, three different styles are shown: a commercial, cotton-meshed net; a homemade, square wire net; and a commercial conical net of wire.

hoop of the net. As far as the depth goes, 12 to 14 inches will suffice. Many home craftsmen use wire mesh for the actual netting. Also, many commercial trotliners, who rely heavily on their scap net, use conical, wire-meshed nets. Why wire? Longevity might be one reason, but mainly it's because crabs can be extracted more easily as they do not tangle in the wire. This is vital to someone working a long trotline of closely-spaced baits, but it's important to the sport crabber, too. Who wants to spend half the day untangling crabs from a net?

In truth, there are places where you *want* the crab to become entangled. One example might be where you are straining to reach a crab, and can't be assured of raising a long, heavy net in an upright position. Consider where you'll be doing your scapping. If you do go to a soft-meshed net, make it one with thick mesh spaced closely together. This will minimize tangling.

Scapping can be done from boat or shore. When you spy a crab, it's best to lower the net slowly until you're no more than a foot away from your target. Water resistance will make the final "swoosh" slower than you think. If the crab is moving, you will have to anticipate his avenue of escape. This just takes practice.

FROM A BOAT. Boats help sportsmen catch more fish, and it's just as true with crabs. You have far more mobility and can search around for crab concentrations. Often, this means nearer or farther from the ocean, depending on recent run-off and where the salt line is. In well protected bays and rivers, a motorless row boat of 12 to 14 feet is all you need. A semi-V hull construction will be more stable than a Jon Boat, which will restrict you to pretty flat waters. On bigger crabbing grounds, like Chesapeake Bay, Delaware Bay, and the lower Hudson River, a rowboat is inadequate and dangerous. Move on up to a 16 to 18 foot outboard, though, and you'll be equipped for a high percentage of crabbing waters.

If you pursue your sport well inland, a bigger boat may be a hindrance. Small Jon Boats or duck boats 10 to 12 feet in length serve many crabbers well, especially on small tidal rivers and backwaters. Have oars or paddles aboard to navigate shallow water, even if you use an outboard.

Pots, trotlines, handlines, scap nets, and traps can all be

Even a small rowboat of 10 or 12 feet can help you catch more crabs. Each trap you set will need its own buoy. Below is one of our traps all rigged and ready to go. We prefer flat, notched buoys to the more commonly used Clorox bottles.

deployed from a boat. The basics of the first two are covered in the next chapter. Here is a little advice on each of the other three techniques when used in conjunction with a boat.

Sport crabbers who boat widely prefer traps. Once baited, the trap is lowered to the bottom and is then marked and held in place with a buoy. Most crabbers use plastic Clorox bottles, but these are very cumbersome to tote around and store (though they make beautiful boat anchors when filled with sand and water). My solution came when I found some sheets of two-inch-thick Styrofoam that someone had discarded. You could also take a cheap cooler and cut it into 10-inch squares. Each piece is notched out on two sides, which provides a means of tying the trap's line on securely, and helps to keep the line coiled around the buoy so wind and tide cannot unravel it. Just remember to leave a little extra slack to allow for a rising tide, or your buoy will disappear into the blue yonder. Where we crab, there are occasionally arguments over people pulling the wrong trap. My father (who likes to argue but not when he's crabbing) therefore got the idea to paint the initial "C" on all our buoys.

Set up a little camp on shore to avoid crowding your small boat with paraphernalia. Between pulls, rig up extra bait, leaving some spare string so it can easily be tied into traps that need it next trip out. It's important to move your traps around. If a trap doesn't produce after a few pulls, move it. If a trap in a particular location catches fire, put four or five more right close by. A good crabber is almost always busy: Checking, moving, adding fresh bait, exploring around the bay, and working at filling that bushel.

Scapping from a boat can be very fruitful, but in certain locations only. By day, the crab is largely a bottom dweller, and bright sunlight might push him even deeper or into the weeds. That's why the best scapping is at night. In the daytime, a boater's best bet is to look for crabs latched onto bridge abutments, docks, and old pilings. Crabs have a definite penchant for hanging onto things, though Lord knows why. Even when you're using traps, from shore or boat, bring along a scap net. It will almost always mean a few extra crabs at the end of the day, though probably not a whole bushel by itself.

Handlining, covered earlier in this chapter, is done in the same basic fashion from a boat as from shore. Again, it is often combined with trapping to liven up those dull moments between pulls. An extra oar or just a stick laid bow-to-stern just inside the gunnel will serve to hold the three or four lines you might want to fish. A boat anchor, not needed when using traps, becomes useful.

Should you find yourself on windier waters, or places with strong tides, an additional piece of equipment will become necessary: A hook for snatching the lines of your traps or pots. A 6-foot tool handle with any gaff-like hook fastened to the end will serve the purpose.

NIGHT CRABBING. The biggest crabs I've ever caught or seen caught were taken at night. As an example, one day a friend and I were crabbing off a bridge over a small tidal river in Connecticut. It was some time past midnight when we heard a clanking noise. Quite suddenly, two men in a 10-foot Jon Boat drifted down beneath the bridge. When we shined our flashlights down on them, we couldn't believe our eyes. In the aft section of the boat, on the bottom, were two or three enormous crabs, possibly the largest I've ever seen. They were at least eight to nine inches, maybe bigger. But the mystery ship drifted on down before we could really talk to the men. I did notice that they were scapping while using lanterns, the most popular nighttime method. Exactly where or how they caught those monster blue claws was the question we never got to ask.

This prompted me to do some checking. Just what *is* the record blue claw? The biggest one I have heard of, though I could not verify it, is a 9 1/2 incher taken in Virginia. My personal biggest is 8 1/2 inches taken from the Hudson River. If big blue claws approaching these sizes are your game, night is your time. Also, late season seems to produce the biggest crabs, at least in my area.

Just before dark, blue claws often move into shallower water, and can be scapped quite easily by crabbers walking along muddy banks. A dead low tide that has just started to inch in can be deadly at this time. After dark, males–especially big males–seem to become more active. This is most noticeable in summer, when mature males are on the prowl for peelers to mate with. While crabs can and do cover a lot of ground, the propensity to do so increases as the late summer breeding period approaches.

Traps don't work well at all for us at night, at least from solid darkness up to about 3 or 4 a.m. In some places, especially quiet or clear waters with weak tides, I've seen cages go all night without catching a thing. Come the very first hint of light, though, and those same cages

Night crabbing is one of the best ways to fill a bushel basket. The night light pictured here, easily made for around $10, calls for an ordinary sealed beam, a wooden handle and a 12-volt battery, plus several feet of wire. Photo at left shows detail of how the beam is attached to the end of the pole. A three-pronged metal clip is nailed to the end of the handle. Then each prong is soldered to one terminal on the beam. Electrical tape holds the wire from each prong in place. Also tape the wire securely at several points along the handle.

might come up with three or four crabs apiece. Crabs have excellent eyesight, and perhaps night negates this important means of finding the bait. However crabs are also thought to have a keen sense of smell. All I can make of it is that the peak of crab *feeding* activity might be from about 4 to 9 a.m. Consistently, this is when our traps catch the most blue claws. Sometimes, 9 a.m. to noon can also be fairly good, and for sure, you can catch *some* crabs all day long.

Even if they aren't feeding heavily, crabs do a lot of moving around after dark. During the witching hours, good scapping teams can fill not just a bushel but a garbage can. The required outfit is a boat, a good lantern and a long scap net. Perhaps ideal for night scapping is a team of three individuals. One becomes the oarsman or motorman. Another holds the light. The third does the scapping. By prowling the inland waterways, tidal rivers, and bays, crabbers can learn where the most crabs move at night. The crab is simply spotted with the lantern and netted. Some teams work an area by rotating the lantern like a beacon, covering every foot of water.

Crabs like to swim on or near the surface at night, and this idiosyncrasy is largely what makes night scapping so productive. Once spotted, they are not difficult to

Crabbing gear is simple but nobody ever said it was compact. Shown are: one overnight pot, several traps of different design, tongs for culling, a bushel basket and some small stuff that we carry in the little canvas bag.

capture. Most crabbers agree that the night hours yield more males than females. It is the role of the male in nature to seek out the female, and perhaps night is when the courting blue claw is most active.

Surface-swimming crabs will account for only part of your catch. Many crabs swim along the bottom at night. These bottom skulkers are much more challenging targets. Yet it has been my observation that this is how to get the biggest crabs. Big Jimmies, the real tanks over seven inches, seem to stay on bottom even at night.

The 10-foot aluminum net described under scapping is

usually appropriate. A strong, hand-held lantern with a 12-volt battery is satisfactory, but the stronger the light, the more crabs you'll catch. The accompanying photo shows an excellent rig for night scapping. Here an automobile sealed beam has been attached to the end of a 5-foot tool handle. Two hot wires and one ground wire are attached to the beam, and are taped along the shaft of the handle. The wires are connected to a 12 volt car battery (in this case with screws, though alligator clips can also be employed). Bill Branciforte, who uses this light for night scapping on both Great South and Barnegat Bays, says that 12 to 14 gauge wire is good.

If you're not finding crabs in the open at night, look for clumps of weeds (especially eelgrass) in shallow water. A person in waders or hip boots walks through the weeds, kicking, while the light person focuses his beam along the opposite end of the weeds. Crabs will sometimes come darting out. Blue claws may also go very far upstream in a tidal creek at night, possibly for the actual mating process. It pays to explore way back in.

Finally, expect to see a few good nights then a few bad nights. Check every day if you live near the water and take advantage of the spurts.

OTHER METHODS. In spring, the relatively small percentage of adult females that went unbred the previous season get one more chance. You can entice these anxious females with either of two methods.

Jimmy potting is practiced in the Chesapeake mainly during the last two weeks of May. It may work earlier or later at different latitudes. It means simply baiting a pot with two or three big, live Jimmies. The starry-eyed sooks-to-be readily come in hoping for a fling. You can use either commercial or sport pots, as described in the next chapter. You can even try tying a big male into a box trap. We've done that and it has sometimes worked even in summer and fall.

If this sounds like sexploitation, here's an even dirtier trick. Tie a long, stout string on a big Jimmy, and let him swim around. The sometimes coy females are easy marks in the spring. When your Jimmy picks one up, you pull him in, steal the peeler he is carrying, and send him back out. It's been noted that you can only frustrate your macho man five or six times before he stops picking up "wives." Then you have to tie on a fresh stud.

Rod and reel baited with fish or worm is a viable crabbing method. It works much better from a boat, as the crabs are more likely to hold on. A 6-foot scap net is necessary.

Yet another method is seining. It's especially productive in small bays, tidal pools, or other places where crabs can be concentrated in fairly shallow water. Two people are needed. Don't forget hip

When you're setting traps from a boat or from shore, a nice thing to have along is a grappling hook. It's saved many a trap for us. We use a large treble hook and a 6-ounce bank sinker attached to the end of a 20-foot length of 3/8-inch polypropylene.

boots or bathing suit, and sneakers or sandals to protect your feet. Also check on the legality of this method in your area.

MISCELLANEOUS GEAR. The main items are covered throughout the book, and especially in this chapter. When my father and I go crabbing, the only other thing we bring is a small canvas bag with a few odds and ends. A ball of string will last two seasons, and will be used for tying in bait and making handlines. Carry, also, some wire and a pair of wire cutters. This is for making repairs on traps or pots. Four-ounce sinkers for weighting a trap can sometimes save the day in strong currents. One or two-ounce sinkers are usually plenty for weighting a handline. Don't forget rags! Crabbing is messy. Carry a stout sheath knife, but make it a cheap one. The grating of wire mesh and the salty water will abuse it. A cooler with ice is sometimes indicated: For food and beverages in hot weather, and for transporting crabs home if it's going to be a long, hot drive.

It's a good idea to tote two baskets: A bushel and a half-bushel. The small one is handy for carrying around as you work your handlines or make "pulls" out in the boat. As the small one fills, empty it into the bigger one on shore. Usually, the owner of your local fish store will provide you with a basket or two.

Our "necessary" bag. Wire, string and a few tools are all you really need for this prosaic pastime.

Some crabbers swear by a red ribbon tied into a trap, claiming it attracts crabs. Tie it from the top so it dangles down to just above the bait.

FOUR

Getting Serious – Potting & Trotlining

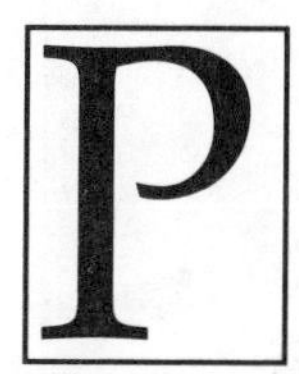

otting is the method that now accounts for the greatest share of the commercial harvest of hard crabs. A pot differs from the traps we have so far discussed in one important way: The crabs come in but usually cannot get out. Thus a pot only has to be checked once a day. Additionally, it's larger than a trap to hold way more crabs, more foul-proof, and much more efficient overall.

Commercial potters may run 100-200 pots at a time. Since the pots can weigh over 30 pounds when filled with crabs and dripping seaweed, a hydraulic "pot puller" is used by many. Few sport crabbers will want to get this involved, and fewer still will want to throw their back out lifting pots by hand. However more and more sport crabbers are using this professional attack to augment their day's catch. Whether you're running traps, handlines, or just scapping, you can set out a few pots when you arrive and check them just before leaving. Two dozen crabs in one pot is not unusual.

Recently, a number of sport pots have begun to appear on the market, and you should check these out. They are lighter and less expensive than the standard commercial models. Last year, I even saw a "mini" sport pot. It was

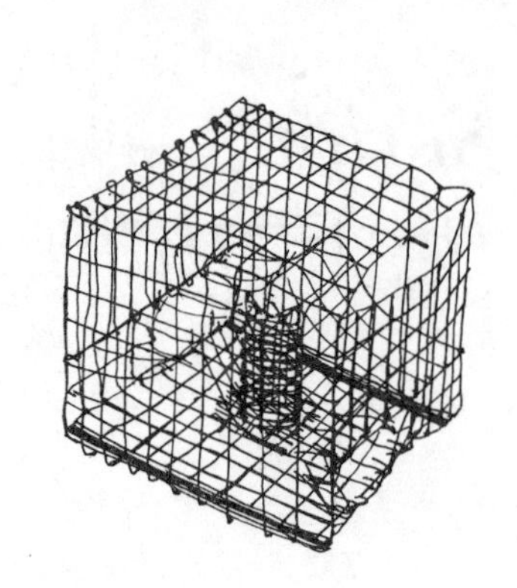

A rigged and ready-to-go "sport" crab pot. It's just a little smaller on each side than a standard commercial pot. As with all crab pots the "bait box" is in the center. The bait is inserted into this cylindrical unit from the bottom; the bait is held in place with any type of a flap, sometimes just a plastic coffee can lid.

In the top illustration, the "door" through which the crabs are dumped out is slightly ajar. Here to the right, that door is being pried open. Of course the door is just one side of the pot with the top end of that side featuring an open seam. Usually, a small clip combined with a short elastic piece keeps the door closed.

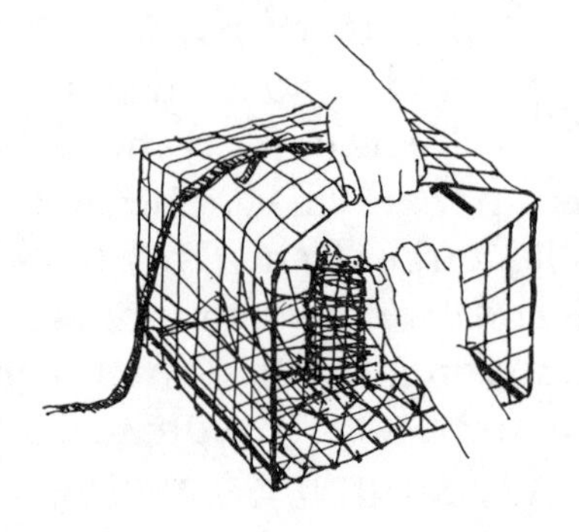

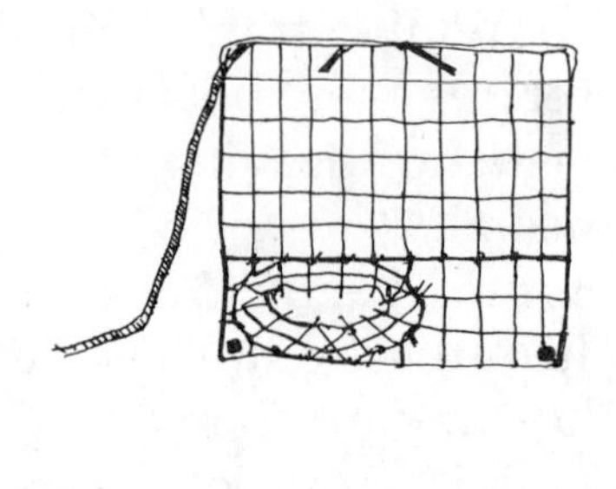

Crab pots have two, three, or four "funnels", through which the crabs enter. These are always located towards the bottom of the pot. The pot shown on this page has two funnels. A close-up of one of them is shown to the left.

no bigger than a small box trap.

A big advantage to pots is that the crabs can't get at the bait too well, and certainly can't walk off with it. Also, since the bait is enclosed, much softer stuff like fish chunks can be used. Commercial potters have a marked preference for alewives and blueback herring. But you can use whatever you've got.

A great many professional crabbers make some of their own pots. It's not worth it, though, unless you make quite a few, since you have to buy rolls of wire in bulk to save anything. Two-inch mesh is generally called for for the main pot, while 1/4-inch mesh is used for the bait box. Even with this zinc-treated steel (much more costly than chicken wire), pots may not last more than a season. In waters of lighter salinity, pots last much longer. Between seasons, some crabbers tar their pots to ward off further deterioration.

Pots should be kept clean and free of weeds and other obstructions. Crabs are said to avoid pots they can't see into. This is one drawback to the newer, vinyl-coated pots. They resist corrosion better but they become fouled with debris more easily.

Warm Thoughts In Winter

In winter, growing tired of chicken,
(all that grease and finger lickin')
oh, how we long for May and June
when blue crabs come to our lagoon.

Through the chilly weeks we wait,
saving necks and backs for bait
to trap them. And, with any luck
it isn't hard to fill a bucket.

Crusted jimmies with pop-top tails,
feisty sooks with painted nails,
packing sweet white meat that makes
eyes-bigger-than-my-belly cakes.

Onions, crumbs, paprika, parsley—
everything but crab used sparsely.
Two, three hundred crabs a year
consumed with love and ice-cold beer.

Robert Keay, Clearwater, Florida

TROTLINES. Trotlining holds much potential for the sport crabber who wants to catch crabs by the bushel (or bushels) but also have a lot of fun. It should be of interest to any who might want to go "semi-pro" and sell a few bushels a week, since it does not require a large, initial investment (it does require a boat).

Trotlining was the primary commercial method from the 1800's right up to the 1930's, when the patented crab pot started taking over. Nonetheless, trotlines are still run for profit, in upper Chesapeake Bay for example.

A trotline is nothing more than a long line, resting on bottom and anchored at both ends, to which a series of baits are tied at intervals of about two to six feet. Trotlines are almost always worked from a boat. Commercial crabbers run one, two, or possibly three lines up to about two-thirds of a mile in length. Sport crabbers should certainly start with a much shorter length until they get the hang of it. Even 50 yards will be a lot at first.

The line itself is usually 1/8 to 3/16 of an inch in diameter, and is made of hemp, cotton, nylon, or other material. "The longer the line, the heavier the anchor" is one rule of thumb. Just remember *not* to attach the anchor directly to the line. Rather, the anchor should lead to a buoy on a separate rope. At each end of the main line, a short length of chain (or other type of weight) is spliced in to keep the line on bottom. Again, the length of the main line and bottom currents will dictate how heavy this weight should be. The end of this chain is then attached by a separate rope to the same buoy as is the main anchor.

Crabs often seem more reluctant to enter pots and traps in spring than in summer. Try handlines or trotlines when you're seeing crabs but not catching them in your traps.

The bait is tied directly to the main line, or to "snoods," droppers that run off the main line. The snood method is less popular today than it once was. Highly preferred for trotline bait is pieces of eel. Its elongated shape makes eel easy to tie on and it is extremely tough, so the crabs have a hard time polishing it off. Tough animal parts like beef nose, and tough trash fish are also put to work. Trotlines can be baited up days ahead of time by making up a barrel of very salty brine (the "pickle") into which the entire line is coiled. If the pickle is made just right, in terms of its preservative capacities, one trotline of baits can be used may days in a row. Your pickle will be right when it floats an egg.

Professionals rig their boats with a beam that extends out beyond the gunnel. The line is yanked up with a gaff,

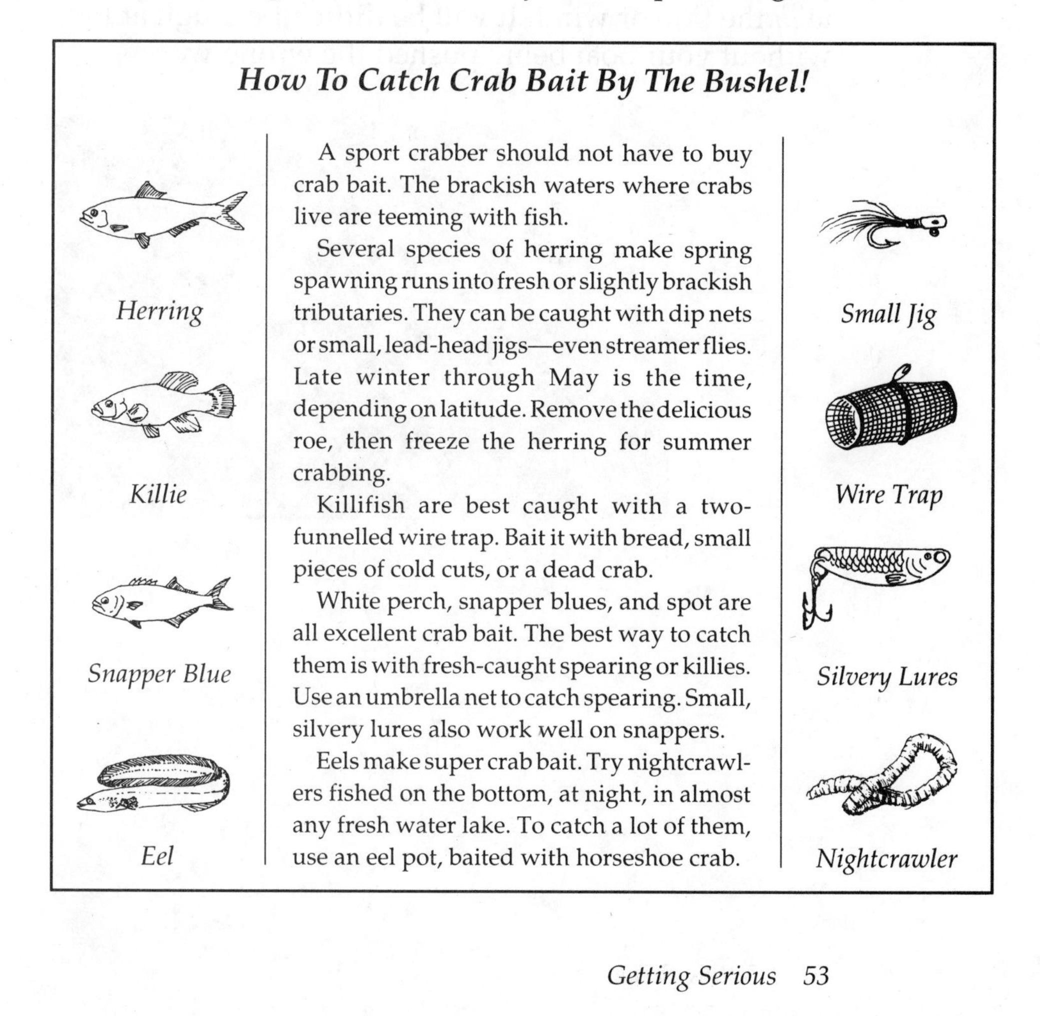

How To Catch Crab Bait By The Bushel!

A sport crabber should not have to buy crab bait. The brackish waters where crabs live are teeming with fish.

Several species of herring make spring spawning runs into fresh or slightly brackish tributaries. They can be caught with dip nets or small, lead-head jigs—even streamer flies. Late winter through May is the time, depending on latitude. Remove the delicious roe, then freeze the herring for summer crabbing.

Killifish are best caught with a two-funnelled wire trap. Bait it with bread, small pieces of cold cuts, or a dead crab.

White perch, snapper blues, and spot are all excellent crab bait. The best way to catch them is with fresh-caught spearing or killies. Use an umbrella net to catch spearing. Small, silvery lures also work well on snappers.

Eels make super crab bait. Try nightcrawlers fished on the bottom, at night, in almost any fresh water lake. To catch a lot of them, use an eel pot, baited with horseshoe crab.

and laid on the beam between guides or on rollers. Thus as the crabber works his line, the baits with crabs clutched on are forced up to the surface; they are usually scap netted just before they break surface. It's not hard to rig something like this up. But if you can't, the line can be worked the old fashioned way: hand over hand. A neophyte will almost surely need a partner.

Trotliners, like *all* successful crabbers, start out early. Most of their work is done between 4 a.m. and 11 a.m. This is the best time.

The beginner, in particular, is advised to work his line *with* the tide or wind. It will be difficult enough at first without your boat being pushed the wrong way.

FIVE

All About Softshells

The tide moved in silently, disturbing neither man nor beast. The train clacked and clammored, with an ear-ringing report. The tide left a clean, sweet smell of salt and eelgrass. The train left a putrid trail of billowing, diesel smoke. The tide gently rocked my little rowboat, nearly lulling me back to sleep. The train listed and pitched, making it impossible for the people inside to even read let alone drink coffee. The tide was on schedule for the hundred millionth year. The 8:03 was late again.

And so of a soft August morning, we, each, had made our choices. The commuters riding the Hudson line had chosen the big city and the near certainty of financial reward, but also the deadening pace of commuting and the subservience to corporate masters. I had chosen the freedom of the river, but also the uncertainties of a career as an outdoor writer. The sand bar that had walked out from a sea of *Phragmites* six hours earlier was now nearly covered. The great blue heron disappeared to its mysterious, high tide netherland and I picked up my scap net to see what was about.

Back those many years ago, before I really understood the life cycle of the blue claw, softshells were always a great mystery to me and my crabbing buddies. How come we never caught any? "Probably don't feed after they've moulted" we correctly theorized. How come we don't see them in the mud along the bank? "Maybe they bury themselves in the mud at moult time," we mused incorrectly. Could you simply keep a hardshell and wait for it to moult into a softshell? We had no answer for that one though we thought we might be on the right track.

High tide in the Hudson lapped up against the shore, laying thick mats of eelgrass at the feet of wind-bent white ash and evening primrose. As I skulked along the

Beneath or alongside of modern bridges or trestles you may find the remnants of long-gone bridges. The rotting pilings of these ancient spans will harbor both hard crabs and doublers. Doublers like to hide among wood or rock rubble.

water's edge in hip boots, I finally spotted a very big crab within net's reach and partially hidden under a rock. Carefully, I plotted its sideways escape route and made my thrust. Success! But when I hoisted the net up over my shoulder and safely onto land it felt heavier than it should have. I turned the scap net upside down and the big male tumbled out trailing small bits of weed. Only then was I to notice a little surprise: a small female apparently being carried by the much bigger male.

I separated the two and guessed at their sizes. The male was about 6 1/2 to 7 inches long while the female was about 4 inches. Since they were my first two crabs of the day, I tossed them into my empty bushel, vaguely thinking that later I would release the female. Then I got the notion that the big male might kill the female so I placed her in a small bucket with a little water.

I went about my business of checking my baited traps, and as the action was good, I didn't get a real break for a couple of hours. Finally, while relaxing on shore, I happened to peek into the pail holding the small female. But now there were two crabs! And there was no one around to have played a trick on me. Now I can be pretty gullible, but I had taken enough biology to know that spontaneous generation of a new organism was in that same medieval bag of tricks as alchemy. I poked at the "two crabs" and one was, as I suspected, a cast shell. The other, very much alive and wiggling slightly, was a perfect little softshell. I'd shed out my first crab! Naturally, that softshell made a delicious dinner later on, but the real marvel was the perfection of the cast shell. From above, it looked exactly like a real crab, right down to the finest detail. I've since been fooled many times by "dead crabs" that lay on shore and turned out to be exoskeletons left behind by blue claws.

The mysteries of the blue claw began to unfold in subsequent months as I studied up on its life history. With enlightenment came more and more softshell suppers.

As partially discussed in Ch. 1, crabs moult many times during their lives. Since their "skeleton" is on the outside, they have to do so in order to grow. What interests crabbers, and gourmands, are the moults that occur *after* that time when the crab is about 3 1/2 inches in length. This

Crabbing Regulations are often complex. Following are the addresses you should send to to find out about seasons and any restrictions in some cases. Contact the town clerk where you plan to crab.

NEW YORK: NYS Dept. of Environmental Conservation, Bureau of Shellfisheries, Building 40, SUNY, Stony Brook, NY 11794

FLORIDA: Shellfish Administration, Dept. of Natural Resources, 3900 Commonwealth Blvd., Tallahassee, FL 32399

CONN: Dept of Environmental Protection, Marine Fisheries, Great Neck Road, Waterford, CT 06385

NJ: Dept. of Environmental Protection, Bureau of Shellfisheries, 401 East State Street, Trenton, NJ 08625

MARYLAND: Dept. of Natural Resources, Tawes State Office Building, Annapolis, MD 21401

DELAWARE: Division of Fish & Wildlife, P.O. Box 1401 Dover, DE 19903

RI: Division of Fish & Wildlife, Washington Cty. Govt. Center, Tower Hill Road, Wakefield, RI 02879

MASS: Division of Marine Fisheries, 100 Cambridge Street, 19th Floor, Boston, MA 02202

VIRGINIA: Virginia Resources Comm., 2401 Washington Ave., Newport News, VA 23607

NC: Div. of Marine Fisheries, 3411 Arendell Drive, Moorehead City, NC 28557

GEORGIA: Coastal Resources Division, Shellfish Section 1200 Glynn Ave., Brunswick, GA 31523

SC: Dept. of Fish & Wildlife, Marine Resources Division, P.O. Box 12559, Charleston, SC 29412 might leave about four more moults in the female or about eight more in the male. Just after it has moulted or "shed", the blue crab is completely soft and also completely good to eat. It remains so for about 12 to 18 hours. After this it goes to the papershell stage, when its new shell begins to stiffen somewhat. Some people still like them at the early papershell stage, and believe me, that's what you get more often than not in inferior seafood stores and restaurants. However, I like my softshells truly soft.

So, in the mature stages of a crab's life you have several potential shots at a softshell, each one lasting about a day after a moult. How do you catch them at the moment of truth? You certainly can go buy them, and some tips on marketing for softshells are later presented. But with a little knowledge and the right implement, you can save that hefty price per softshell at the fish store

Let's first talk about incidental catches, like my own serendipitous encounter on a back bay of the Hudson River.

A few days before a female crab is about to moult for her final time, she will be picked up (literally) by a male. The male will "cradle carry" her for up to several days. At this point they are called "doublers" or less commonly, "buck and rider." The lady gets the free ride because the one and only love affair she can ever have must occur immediately after her final moult. Nature thus arranges it that the male be present, and very few healthy females go unbred.

The female I caught in the Hudson that day was as "rank" as they come—ready to moult. Thus, anytime you catch doublers you can count on the female—if she's still an immature Sally—moulting sometime soon. It might be an hour, it might be a few days; you might even catch one "busting", actually in the process of moulting. The problem is, if she isn't actually busting out at the moment

While night crabbing from a boat can be very fruitful, sneaking along the shoreline after dark (facing page) can also pay dividends. You may find peelers in the weedy shallows and you may also see doublers paddling along looking for a mating place.

you catch her, how do you keep her alive long enough to moult? She must be in water, yet that water must be oxygenated. I have friends who have successfully shed out rank (or "red sign") crabs in oxygenated home aquariums. I also know a few bait dealers who have used their aerated tanks for this purpose. If you live near the shore, you can make up a simpler version of the professional crabber's "shedding float". This is little more than a slatted, wooden trap that floats in the water. Put in your red sign crabs, check the floats often and eventually you'll come up with softshells. I've watched this being done on Smith Island in Chesapeake Bay, and if you are interested in shedding out your own crabs you owe it to yourself to make the ferry ride out to this island and talk to the residents whose lives literally revolve around crabbing.

You can also try a large bait bucket aerated with those little battery-run gadgets most commonly used to keep fish bait like shiners alive. Again, if it was an immature female from a pair of doublers, you shouldn't have too long to wait.

Where do you find doublers? Sometimes the male, carrying the obliging female, will crawl into a baited trap. This happens very infrequently by my experience. Sometimes doublers will also hang onto the side of a bridge abutment or piling. Then, you can just scap the pair up. Any place where there is rock or rubble in the water is a dandy place to look. The doublers will often be seen half hidden and a skilled scapper can have his at-bat. Every once in a while, the female of a doubled pair will be a true softshell. Then, naturally, your work has already been done for you.

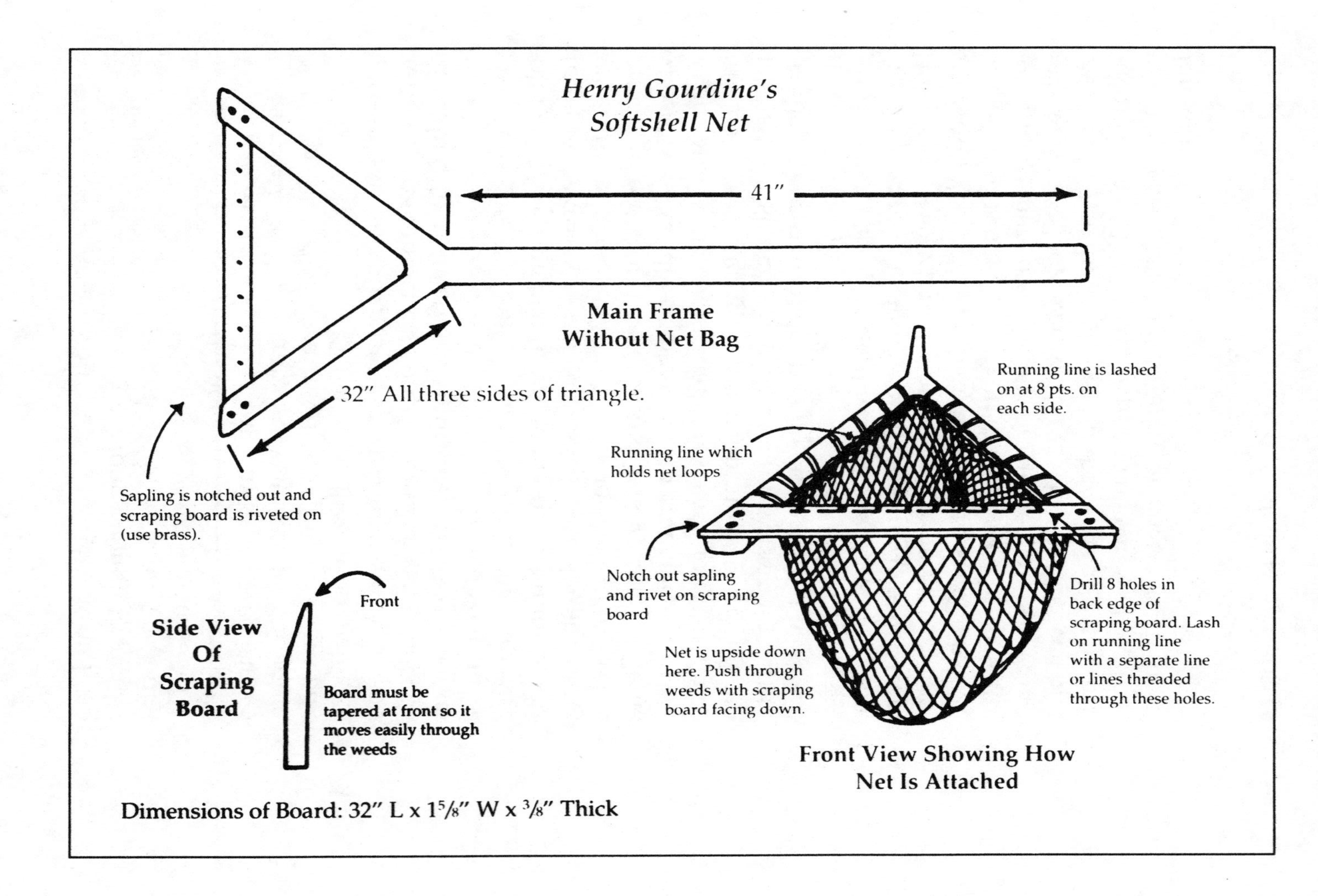
Henry Gourdine's
Softshell Net
41″
Main Frame
Without Net Bag
32″ All three sides of triangle.
Sapling is notched out and
scraping board is riveted on
(use brass).
Running line is lashed
on at 8 pts. on
each side.
Running line which
holds net loops
Notch out sapling
and rivet on scraping
board
Drill 8 holes in
back edge of
scraping board. Lash
on running line
with a separate line
or lines threaded
through these holes.
Net is upside down
here. Push through
weeds with scraping
board facing down.
Front View Showing How
Net Is Attached
Front
Side View
Of
Scraping
Board
Board must be
tapered at front so it
moves easily through
the weeds
Dimensions of Board: 32″ L x 1⁵⁄₈″ W x ³⁄₈″ Thick

By the preceding methods, you can crab a good long time and not dine too often on softshells. If this delicacy is near heaven to you or your tablemates, better approach it the way the pros do, although on a less grand scale.

Crabs about to moult, both doublers and individual crabs, often go to thick beds of eelgrass (*Zostera marina*) to do it. This underwater grass is subtidal, meaning its roots are covered with water even at lowest tide. Often this aquatic grass isn't visible until near low tide. Where it is present, large mats of it will routinely wash up on shore as its root system is apparently unfirm. It grows very thick and affords superb cover for not only moulting crabs but a whole array of marine critters.

A large percentage of softshells that reach market are taken by commercial "scrapers" who, using boats, pull a kind of a dredge through beds of eelgrass. You can work the eelgrass, too, without a boat and without a scrape. All you need is a pair of hip boots or old sneakers and a special homemade net.

The softshell net illustrated in the drawings was designed by Henry Gourdine, who has been fishing the Hudson River commercially for about 75 years. It's very unlikely that you can buy such a net; the closest I've seen is the scalloper's push net which is also worked in eelgrass and which might work for crabbers. To make one will take a little effort, but once done you should be eating softshell crabs about ten times more often. The one requirement will be that eelgrass beds are somewhere present in the waters you crab (sadly, pollution has decimated the eelgrass in some waters). The dimensions and basic construction are given along with the drawings.

Operation of the net is very simple. Using hip boots or just an old pair of sneakers and rolled up trousers or shorts, wade into the shallows where eelgrass is waving enticingly in the current. Even at lowest tide its root system will be submerged. Thus, you'll have to wade to get at it. On the other hand, at high tide, the beds of eelgrass may very well be completely covered and just not findable or workable. Best to time your foray so it's between about one hour short of dead low and for two hours thereafter.

Using both hands, hold the net down away from you and at about a 45 degree angle to the water, the beveled edge of the scraping board facing up. The bottom of the scraping board does not necessarily have to touch the sea floor. Now just push the net through the weeds, ending each push in an upward thrust. You might want to be taking a few steps as you do this. After each push or two, inspect your net to see what you've come up with. Try to wear a belt, to which you can hang a small bucket for your catch. You might want to wear heavy gloves to make removing the hard crabs easier.

You'll definitely pick up a few hardshells, oftentimes big males that have come to the beds seeking out rank females. What you'll primarily get will depend somewhat on the time of year. Along with a few hard crabs, you'll get a few true softshells, as well as a few doublers, the females of which (if they're still Sallies) will be rank and which you can shed out as described earlier on. You'll also pick up a few male and female crabs nearing their moult but not doubled up, and if you can read crabs—described in Ch. 1—you can try to keep these red signs until they shed out. Finally, you'll pick up a few papershells and buckrams, and it is advised that you throw these latter two back.

If you're not able to make a softshell net, you'll have to mainly rely on lucky encounters with softshells, as we've rambled on about. In either case, any increased success in obtaining softies will likely only heighten your craving for them. As a result, you'll probably buy more than ever

Some Possible Effects Of Salinity On Blue Claw Crab Behavior

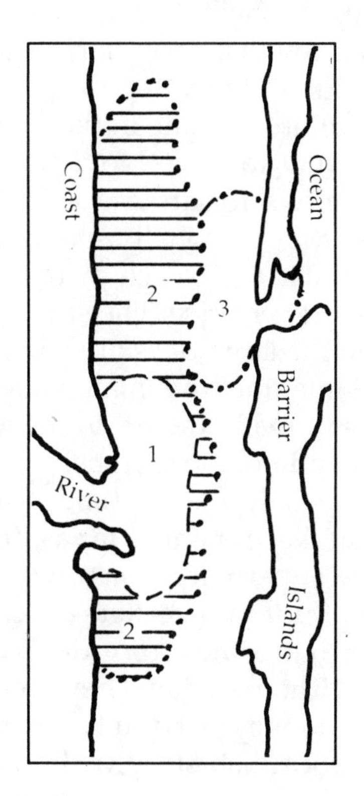

Crabbers can benefit from knowing that Blue Claws will be in waters of different salinities at different stages of life.

In late spring, both males and females migrate towards water of lesser salinity. Some studies indicate that the actual mating process (concentrated in late summer) occurs in very fresh water: 8 parts per thousand salt or less. In fall, most females migrate seaward to far more saline waters. Males move to deeper holes and channels where salinities are somewhat higher.

It's thought that 15 ppt is an optimal salinity for overall blue claw growth. Bigger crabs definitely come from these fresher waters. Crabs will still be found nearer the ocean, but they will invariably be smaller. However, they may also be meatier than crabs from fresher waters, so there are trade-offs.

Droughts can have a dramatic impact on crab movements. In years of light run-off, crabs may be highly concentrated around the mouths of fresh water rivers (#1). This can make for some fantastic crabbing if you're in the right spot. When run-off is heavy, crabs may be more scattered (#2). When run-off is very heavy, pure fresh water might actually chase crabs away from river mouths (#1), and you may have to look nearer the ocean (#3). The salinity factor is discussed in many other parts of the book.

at the fish store. It's a no-win situation, but one of the more pleasant ones.

Prices for fresh softshells will vary widely. In early season, late March through April, softshells will first come on the market and will be priced with a very sharp pencil. As they become more abundant thereafter, the price will come down, only to once more escalate in the final weeks of the softshell season in October or November. You might get lucky and see them for around a buck apiece, and that's the lowest I've personally chanced upon them. More typical is $1.50 to $2.50 each, with the larger ones commanding the higher price. The smaller ones are called "hotels" while the large ones are sometimes called whales or slabs. Sometimes the smaller ones are actually preferred. It doesn't really matter to me as long as the crab is truly a soft and not a papershell.

Go to a good fish store and touch the crabs if that's feasible. If they're crinkly, you can keep them as far as I'm concerned. Buying seafood in a supermarket has always sent me to bed unhappy, if not unfed. The clerks there just don't have the expertise that comes from dealing with seafood and nothing else 15 hours a day. They don't know how to buy, very often, and they just don't seem to use enough ice. Find a good local fish store with nice friendly people and then be monogamous in your seafood purchases. Shellfish are extremely perishable; trust only the pros.

The friendly fish store people we hope you'll encounter will almost always clean the softshells to make them "pan ready." You may find this an advantage since this is a procedure about which some are going to be squeamish. If you obtain your own, you're just going to have to do it yourself.

I take a large, sharp, chef's knife and with one swift blow cut off the entire front section of the crab, including the mouth, eye parts, and presumably, the brain. Although I have no biological verification of it, this seems to kill the softshell instantly and to be the most humane way to dispatch a still-alive softshell. I should note that I do find it acceptable to buy dead (and sometimes precleaned) softshells from a very good seafood store. After this first step, my own approach to cleaning the softshell digresses somewhat from accepted practice.

When your traps start rusting out, don't toss 'em. Just switch the parts around. They're interchangeable!

The softshell pundits tell you to pick up the lateral spine on each end and pry out the finger-like "dead-man" or gills. The spines are then returned to their original position and no further cleaning of the inside of the crab is necessary, they will tell you. However this approach leaves most of the innards still in the crab. To be perfectly blunt, softshell or no softshell, I don't like eating guts. I pry open the abdominal apron and peel back the top shell just as if I was cleaning a hard crab. But I stop short of actually removing the apron and shell. Rather, I leave it attached as I clean and probably wash out all the soft material. Then I carefully fold back the top shell, and—consistent with the pundits—tear off the apron and discard it. The crab is then ready to cook.

My advice is that you avoid ordering softshell crab in questionable eating establishments. Oftentimes, the short order chefs in such places just don't know how to clean or prepare softshells, or distinguish true softshells from papershells. I've found Chinese restaurants to be especially negligent in this regard. By all means, order softshells in a good restaurant whose level of quality you are familiar with. In anything but a top restaurant, hope for the best but expect the worst.

Fresh crab meat is available or at least orderable year round, but softshells are truly seasonal. Crabs just don't moult in the winter time. No moulting, no fresh softshells. I should say that crabs from Gulf of Mexico waters may indeed moult in winter and softshells may possibly be available down there in the winter. Up north where I live, they are not. Ergo, a nagging yen for softshell crab after early November will have to be sated via a trip to the frozen food section of the supermarket.

Crabs, like many gamefish, hate bright sunlight. On bright days, shade in almost any form can spell better crabbing.

Although frozen softshells are certainly not available in all stores at all times, it turns out that this market is quite a large one. I checked a couple of different good supermarkets near me and they did not have frozen softshells. I was told, though, that they could be special-ordered.

Frozen softshells always come pre-cleaned and pan ready, and may even be breaded and/or seasoned to make your job easy.

SIX

Keeping, Cleaning & Cooking Crabs

As most people know, shellfish deteriorate very quickly after they die. That's why it's most important to keep your crabs alive until you get them home. It's generally agreed that crabs can be cooked and eaten for up to four hours after they die, *if* they're kept cold. To be perfectly safe, though, discard any dead crabs and refuse to buy any that are dead.

By the way, when you buy cooked crabs in a restaurant or fish store, you can tell if they were alive when they were cooked. Simply pick the crab (or lobster) up and see how the claws sit. If they sit in a fairly rigid position the crab was alive when cooked. If they sort of sag limply downward, the crab was dead before being cooked

There are two good methods I know of for keeping crabs alive and healthy during the day, while crabbing. One is to keep them in a bushel basket out of the sun. Another is to keep them in a burlap bag that has been thoroughly soaked in water. Ideally, the bag should be dangling in the water, from boat or shore. A tight rope, knotted around the bag's top, will keep crabs from escaping.

If you do keep your crabs in a bushel, or in a burlap bag

out of the water, dip it in the water frequently during the day. Some crabbers place a large rock in the bottom of the basket, then place the basket (containing crabs) in the shallows. This is fine, as long as you keep moving it ahead of the rising tide. In any case, keep a wet piece of burlap or wet rags draped over the basket.

Crabs *should not* be kept in any container filled with water. Oxygen depletion will quickly kill them. If you have a long ride home, or if it's especially hot, put the crabs in a dry cooler on top of some cracked ice. If a crab dies during the day, remove it from the bushel and put it on ice in a cooler. As long as it hasn't been dead too long it will be fine to eat.

Softshells should be kept separate from hard crabs. Softies can be kept very nicely sandwiched between layers of eelgrass and kept in a cooler or box.

STORING CRABS. Virtually all the food experts I talked to recommend cooking crabs before storing them. The reason is simple: why risk having some of them die on you? If you plan to make a sauce, boil the crabs for two minutes, clean them, and place the pieces in a covered bowl in the refrigerator. Reserve all drippings. For most other recipes, extract the meat, and store in a tightly sealed plastic container in the refrigerator. It will keep for several days. Trust your nose with shellfish! What smells bad is bad.

One more safety tip: in polluted waters, neither the cooking water nor the drippings should be consumed. That's because toxic heavy metals leach out into the water the crabs were cooked in.

CLEANING CRABS. For the vast majority of recipes, you will want to fully cook your crabs. One exception is when you're making certain soups and sauces: You might only want to kill the crabs in boiling water (two minutes) before directly adding the cleaned pieces to the sauce. In most cases, though, clean your cooked, hard-shell crabs according to the photos in this chapter.

Here are a few more tips. First, cooked crabs will be very hot, so let them cool before attempting to clean them. Once you pry open the crab and remove the top shell, you will see a lot of soft material—the innards. The six, crescent shaped and somewhat feathery gills on each side should definitely be discarded. But some gourmets relish the soft material just behind the mouth area. The greenish-yellowish material is the Hepatopancreas. Some people like this "crab butter" spread on toast. However,

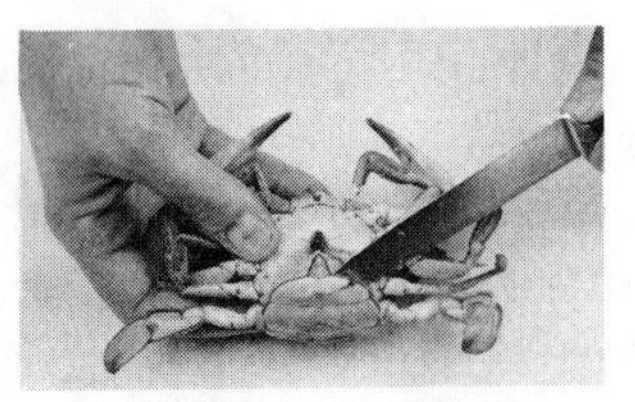

1. Turn crab over and pry open the apron with a sharp knife.

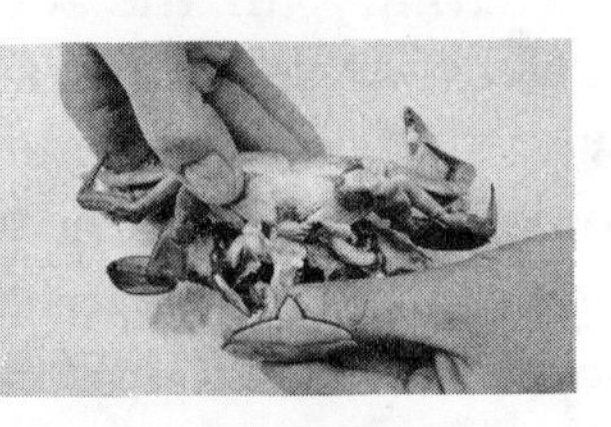

2. Peel apron around, and top shell will come completely off.

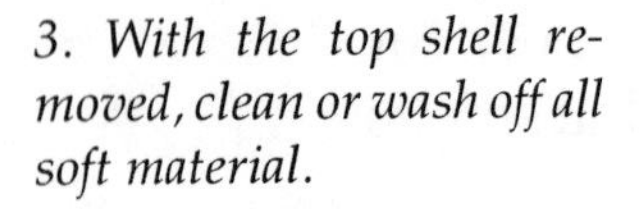

3. With the top shell removed, clean or wash off all soft material.

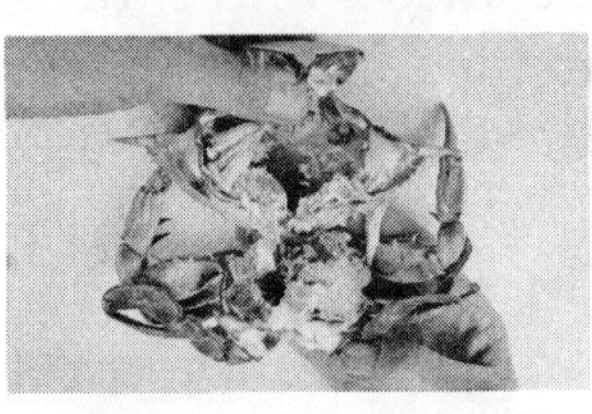

4. Your crab will now look like this.

heavy metals concentrate in a crab's innards, so in waters known for pollution problems, it is usually recommended that you discard the innards. One last thing: Be sure that cooked crabs do not come into contact with anything (tongs, bushel, etc.) that held live crabs. Contamination could result.

FREEZING CRABS. Some crabbers freeze both softshells and hardshells live. As I believe in quickly killing any animal I hunt (which is why I prefer boiling to steaming), I cannot recommend this method. Some experts and cooking schools teach the following procedure. Cook the crabs fully. Then pack the extracted meat from bodies and claws three-fourths full in plastic containers. Fill each container to the brim with water, and freeze at 0° to 5° F. Thaw out slowly in the refrigerator before using. If you do freeze your crab meat in this manner, the water to cover the meat should be salty. The formula should be about one teaspoon of salt per quart of water.

I have not tried this method so I cannot vouch for its effectiveness. Water is said to draw away flavor from the meat, so I have my doubts. When I freeze crabs, I cook and clean them and then place the bodies and claws in a double plastic bag. I do not extract the meat first. However, I prefer fresh crab and do very little of this. Crab spaghetti sauce does freeze well and we usually make up enough containers to last well into winter.

THE ENDLESS CRAB COOKING CONTROVERSY. To steam or boil: The debate rages on, dividing north and south and father and son. The simplest method is to bring a large pot of water to the boil, add your live crabs a few at a time, and boil for about 15 minutes. Crabbers do, of course, add all types of ingredients to the broth: Old Bay Seasoning, mustard, vinegar, bay leaf, salt, cloves, ad infinitum. The supposed intents are to flavorize the meat, decrease kitchen odors, improve the texture of the meat, and so on. However, crabs cooked in plain water seem to taste just fine. Cooked crabs should sit in the water for 15 minutes to "relax the meat", according to one expert chef. He says this also applies to lobster, shrimp and even some meats.

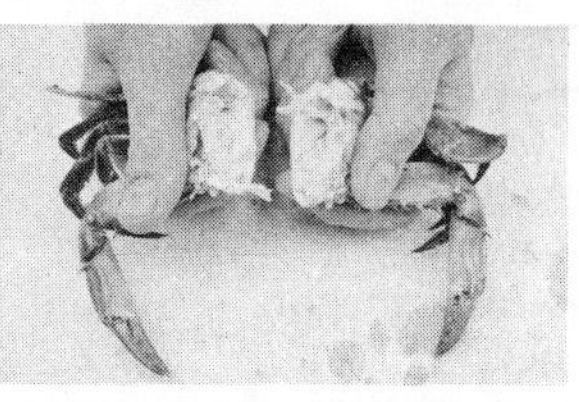

5. Using both hands, break the crab body in half.

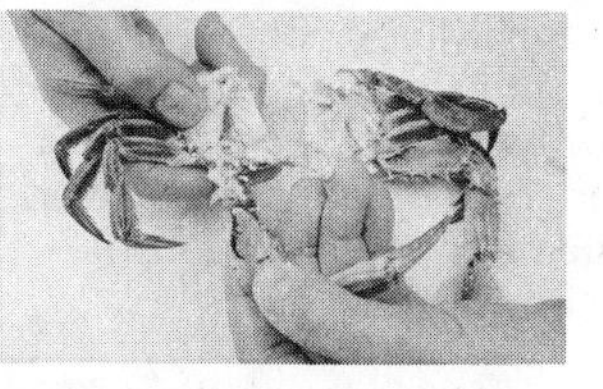

6. Break off the claws and the swimmers; there is good meat in these.

7. Segmented crab will now look like this.

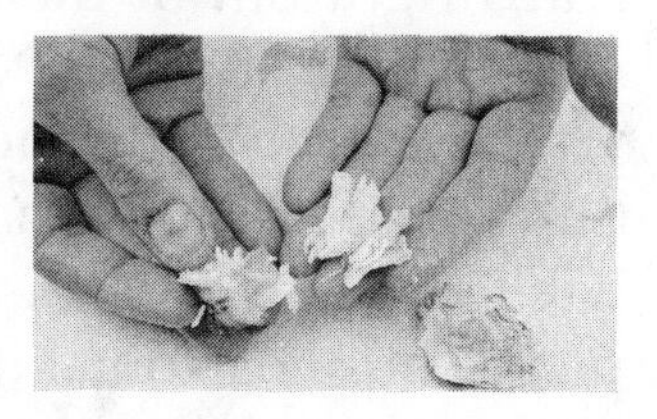

8. Most of the good meat is inside the bodies. Extract carefully using fingers. Crackers will only be needed for large claws.

Steaming, Maryland Style

½ cup seafood seasoning
½ cup salt
3 cups white vinegar
3 cups beer
3 dozen live crabs

Put half of crabs in a large pot with a rack in the bottom. Mix seasonings, vinegar and beer. Pour half over crabs. Add rest of crabs, then rest of mixture. Cover tightly, and steam for about 25 minutes, till crabs turn bright red.

Oh yes: If you can, wash off the crabs with fresh water while they're still alive. A garden hose with a nozzle and a strong spray will do it.

PICKING YOUR CRABS. After you have cleaned your crabs according to the photo sequence, you must decide how you are going to prepare the crab for the table. Let me be effusive in warning you that picking crabmeat too often can get to be very tedious. If your family does a lot of crabbing, and crab eating, I recommend you get them used to eating crabs right out of the shell, perhaps with a little melted butter. Not only do you save yourself potentially hours of picking crabs, but you don't even have to clean the crab. Each diner cleans his own crab and then picks the meat out him or herself. Beyond saving you a lot of work, this is a fine way to enjoy *Callinectes*. Blue claws are delicately flavored, and simple treatments are usually the best.

Scandinavian Crab Boil

20-qt. pot of water
1 bay leaf
20 white peppercorns
1 T. salt
2 T. sugar
½ cup fresh dill
1 T. paprika

Add seasonings to water. Bring to a boil. Add live crabs, a few at a time, returning to boil each time. Boil for about 10 minutes. Turn off heat. Let crabs rest in the hot water at least 15 minutes. *Note:* Reserve some of the cooking water. It can be added to sauces and used in other recipes

Without any doubt, though, there is another whole dimension to crab cookery. The same creature that is so often the centerpiece in a finger-licking orgy off a newspaper tablecloth is just as at home with fine linens and romantic, candle-lit tables. With all the cartilage removed and the work done for your dinner guests, you can tempt them in grand fashion by assembling that pure, white body meat into any one of a myriad of delights. Indeed, blue crab is no stranger to haute cuisine. It figures heavily in the menus of some of the world's greatest restaurants.

But, you'll earn that treat, or the praise that will come with the serving of it. Once you've gotten to photo 7 in the cleaning sequence, you've still two more procedures to go. First, you must pick the meat out, and second, you must go over it a second time to remove any bits of cartilage you missed. Pick an honest quart of crab meat and you'll have had enough of doing that for a month, but what magnificent dining can be wrested from a quart of blue crab.

There is no one right way to pick crabmeat. The claw meat is a little darker, coarser and stronger flavored, and many chefs will not mix it with the white body meat. I use a claw cracker and with a couple of crunches I've usually got the claw meat out. If it's still in one piece, it is (if you like) a "cocktail finger", six of which served with lettuce is a nice appetizer. However, I often will mix claw meat with body meat and the dish I'm making rarely suffers for it.

Professional pickers use very sharp special knives for picking the bodies. Because I play guitar, I hate getting cuts; those band-aids are just brutal. Therefore I avoid using knives and rather, pick the meat out by hand. I usually break each body half in half again and first extract the "backfin" or "lump" meat just inside where the swimming leg was. This is the biggest, most prized morsel in the blue crab. The rest of the body meat will come out in smaller pieces and with greater difficulty.

It is as hard to describe this procedure as it is to illustrate it. Just keep pickin' and you'll get it. The first time you do it, have an experienced hand show you just how it's done.

After you have caught, cleaned and picked the crabs, and even if the day started at 3 a.m., you're not quite ready to align your posterior with your Archie Bunker chair. Now you have to go back through the meat to get out any remaining bits of shell. There will be bits, make no mistake about it. Even a tiny piece of cartilage can mess up a fine crab dish, so this going-over is something I never skip. After this second process, I frequently encounter no shell whatever in the completed dish.

Here's how I scrutinize the already picked out crab meat. I put paper towels on the table. On my right side is

my 2 cup measuring cup with the crab meat. In front of me is a dinner plate. In back of the plate is a bowl for the final, picked-over meat. Finally, to my left is a bowl of warm water and a clean dish towel.

I dump about 1/4 cup of crab meat on the plate and feel through it with my fingers. As I do so, I place it in the empty bowl. As tiny bits of meat and shell stick to my hands, I rinse them off in my finger bowl of water and dry my hands with the towel.

If, for example, it took me an hour to pick the meat out of the crabs, the going-over will normally take only another 20 minutes. It's 20 minutes well spent, since biting into a piece of shell while trying to enjoy a crabcake or whatever, really ruins your day.

As I told you, you earn your crab meat.

For certain recipes, its best to try to keep the white body meat as whole as possible. If for instance, you're making flounder stuffed with crab, the dish will have more eye

You can avoid domestic quarrels by cooking your crabs in the basement or on the patio. A regular 2-burner camp cooking stove will do the job.

"Crab festivals" or "crab bakes" (facing page) are almost as popular as clambakes in some areas. At left, Hudson River educator Christopher Letts has just steamed up a big batch for an environmental group at Kingsland Point Park on the Hudson.

appeal and be more appetizing if the crab filling is mostly lump meat. If the crabs are small or the pickers inexperienced, the body meat may be fairly well shredded. Not to worry—this does nothing to detract from a crab cocktail, or most other recipes calling for picked crab meat.

Experts say that picked crab meat will keep perfectly fine in a refrigerator for a week. No argument. However, I don't push it that far. I use it within no more than five days. Once it's picked, I don't normally freeze it. With the work all done, I'm ready for some good eating. I mean, would you freeze a little lobster meat you had left over? Man, that's self control. Besides, I'm a seasonal cook. I like to both harvest and eat what's in season at the moment.

Remove any dead crabs at once from bushel or cooler. Bacteria rapidly multiply and may end up contaminating other crabs in the batch.

TIPS ON MARKETING. We've already gone over, in Ch.5, some thoughts on buying softshells. Hard crabs can be bought both live (and occasionally cooked) in the shell and in the form of picked meat.

Buying live hard crabs is pretty straightforward. They'll be available most if not all year, but surely between May and October. The charge is always by the dozen and that charge will vary by as much as 300%. $2.50 to $7.00 a dozen is about the range, but in a bad year, large crabs can be as high as $8.00 to $10.00 a dozen.

Crabmeat comes in several forms: fresh (often put up in plastic bags without any liquid and marked fresh), pasteurized, and canned.

Ingredients That Often Go Well With Blue Crabs

Lemon juice	Avocado
Mayonnaise	Onion
Mustard	Milk or cream
Dill weed	Asparagus
Almonds	Butter
Bread crumbs or toast	Pineapple
	Mild curry
Mild cheeses	Paprika (sweet)
Pimentos	Olives
Watercress	Misc. Greens
Tomatoes	Chutney
Parsley	Peaches
Green peppers	

Fresh crabmeat is never inexpensive. Prices will vary widely but eight to sixteen dollars the pound is in the ballpark. It seems high until you've bored yourself to tears picking your own meat. Prices are lowest in summer. Fish store owners tell me the fresh stuff can be gotten all year long (thank the winter dredgers for that) but that in winter it's often extremely expensive.

Don't take old bait home and refreeze it unless it is still ice cold. It could stink up the freezer and probably won't work as well next time anyway.

Finally, in addition to softshells, hard crabs and crab meat, crab lovers can look for several other temptations in the frozen food section of the supermarket. One popular one is deviled crab. Two others are "Crab Miniatures" and "Crab Fingers". Other frozen food dishes incorporate blue crabs in one way or another.

SEVEN

Great Crab Recipes

While lobster is among the most esteemed of all culinary jewels—very much a part of classic french cookery, and now very much a part of American cuisine—some gourmets rate blue crab even a notch higher. In or out of the shell, crab meat is sweet and pleasingly assertive. And while it's not really salty, it brings to your palate an unmistakable taste of the sea.

In all these recipes, crab meat measurements are in dry measure (cups). One pound of crab meat equals about 4 cups. The symbol T. means tablespoon. The symbol tsp. means teaspoon. The symbol lb. means pound. The symbol oz. means liquid ounce. A dash means less than 1/8 tsp. All temperatures are Fahrenheit. One large crab yields about 1/3 to 1/2 cup meat.

CRAB FEAST

This is the simplest and most popular way to enjoy this delectable shellfish. Simply cook the crabs by one of the methods discussed in Ch. 6, allow to cool for ten minutes, then serve on a large tray. Each person extracts the crab meat himself, all you provide is a bowl of bubbly hot butter! Excellent accompaniments are fresh garden tomatoes and ice cold beer. (Allow 3-6 crabs/person, depending on size. You'll actually get about 2 oz. of meat per crab.)

CRAB COCKTAIL

Serves 4

2 cups crab meat
1/2 cup celery
Dash lemon juice
1/2 cup mayonnaise, more or less to taste
Dash salt and pepper

This is probably the second most popular way to serve crab. It's equally simple and satisfying. Chop the celery very fine. Combine with all other ingredients in a mixing bowl. Blend with a fork. Spoon into a cocktail glass on top of a bed of lettuce. Sprinkle with paprika.

Option 1 - Serve inside a halved avocado which has been sprinkled with lemon juice. May also be served in a hollowed out, fresh tomato; in a halved papaya; or atop a slice of pineapple.
Option 2 - Drain liquid from a small can of asparagus tips. Dip one tip at a time in lemon juice. Arrange six tips in a cocktail glass, fill center with crab meat cocktail.
Option 3 - Use any cream puff recipe and bake puffs that are 1 1/2" across (About 1 rounded tsp. dough should do it.) Cut tops off and fill with crab cocktail.
Option 4 - Add small amounts of any or all of these ingredients to the basic crab cocktail recipe: Onion, mushrooms, capers, white wine.

LO-CAL COCKTAIL

Serves 1

2 T. plain yogurt
1 tsp. lemon juice
1 T. safflower oil
1/2 cup flaked crab meat
Salt and pepper to taste.

Blend all ingredients. Serve as under preceding recipe.

CRAB TOAST

Makes about 24 hors d' oeuvres.

2 egg whites, beaten stiff
1/2 cup flaked crab meat, or a little more
Dash Tabasco
1/2 cup mayonnaise

To mayonnaise, add crab and Tabasco. Fold in egg whites. Spoon onto toast rounds made from very thin bread, or onto very thin crackers. Bake at 425° till lightly browned.

CRAB-STUFFED MUSHROOMS

Remove stems from large mushrooms. Sprinkle lightly with white wine. Stuff with flaked crab meat. Place a small circle of herbed butter on top of each mushroom. Place under broiler for a minute or two, or until butter melts.

Herb butter can contain many different ingredients. For each pound of butter, add two whole eggs. This will help produce a nice glaze on the finished product. Soften the butter, add the eggs, and any of these in combination: Brandy, garlic, lemon juice, Tabasco, Worcestershire, parsley, chives, dill, sage, rosemary. *Fresh* herbs are much preferred.

CRAB DIP

7/8 cup mayonnaise
1/2 cup sour cream
1 T. chopped parsley
1 1/2 cups crab meat
1 T. sherry
1 tsp. lemon juice
Salt and pepper to taste
1 tsp. chopped chives

Combine all ingredients. Chill thoroughly before serving. It will be better the next day. Serve on very thin crackers or with thinly sliced crudités.

MOLDED CRAB MEAT SPREAD

2 1/2 cups crab meat
1 10 1/2 oz. can cream of mushroom soup
1 cup very finely diced celery
1 8 oz. package cream cheese
1 small envelope unflavored gelatin
1 small onion, grated
Dash Worcestershire

Heat undiluted soup. Add 3 T. water to gelatin. Add this mixture to soup. Blend into softened cream cheese. Add remaining ingredients. Chill in mold or serving dish. Serve with toast rounds, crackers, or raw vegetables.

CRAB WITH PROSCIUTTO

Makes 6 appetizers

2 cups lump crab meat
Curly parsley for garnish
2 T. chopped parsley
2 tsp. crushed, dry tarragon
2 T. finely chopped onion
4 T. butter
Salt and pepper to taste
6 thin slices of prosciutto, about 6 inches in diameter each.

Saute the onion in melted butter until wilted. Add the crab meat, and heat for a few minutes, tossing gently so as not to break up the lumps. Add the parsley and tarragon and toss again, Add a dash each of salt and pepper. Spoon this mixture onto the slices of prosciutto, folding the ends of the meat over it. Place on a pan and put under the broiler for one minute. Serve with crisp, thin toast.

CRAB SPINACH SALAD WITH EGG

Makes 4 salads

1 12-oz. pkg. fresh spinach
1/2 cup finely-chopped green onion or chives
Dressing (see below)
3 cups lump crab meat
3 hard-cooked eggs, chopped coarsely

Dressing -
Mix 2 T. wine vinegar with 8 T. salad oil. Add 1/2 to 1 tsp. salt (preferably sea salt pounded in a mortar) and freshly ground black pepper to taste. Add 1 T. plus 1 tsp. fresh chopped dill. Blend well.

Master Recipe -
Arrange the spinach leaves in individual serving bowls. Top with crab meat, then chopped onion or chives, and eggs. Spoon dressing over all.

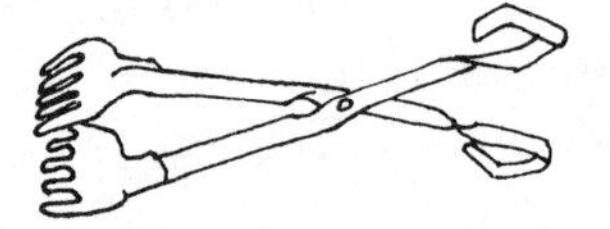

FRUITED CRAB MEAT MOLD

2 tsp. granulated gelatin soaked
  in 1/3 cup grapefruit juice
1 T. tarragon vinegar
1/2 cup mayonnaise
1/2 cup grapefruit pulp
1/2 cup pineapple, crushed
1 cup crab meat

Dissolve gelatin over hot water. Add vinegar, then add this mixture to mayonnaise a little at a time. Blend thoroughly. Mix fruit and crab meat. Add to first mixture. Pack in an oiled mold. Chill. Unmold and serve on lettuce.

DRESSED-UP CRAB MEAT SALAD

Makes 4-6 salads

3 cups crab meat
1 large tomato
1/2 cup Thousand Islands
  Dressing
1 head romaine lettuce
1 avocado
1/4 cup sliced almonds

Remove outer leaves from lettuce head. Take smaller inside leaves and arrange on a platter or on individual serving dishes. Spoon lump crab meat over lettuce. Circle with alternate wedges of tomato and avocado. Sprinkle all lightly with lemon juice. Spoon on dressing to taste. Sprinkle on the almonds. Serves 4 generously as a side dish.

HOT CRAB CANAPES

1 egg yolk
1/4 cup thick white sauce
1 1/2 T. cream
1/4 lb. cheddar cheese, diced
Dash cayenne
1/4 tsp. salt
1/8 tsp. paprika
2/3 cup crab meat,
  flaked and lightly chopped
1/4 tsp. Worcestershire

Beat egg yolk, add seasonings, cheese and white sauce. Cook until smooth, stirring constantly. Add cream. Add crab meat. Spread on canapes (sauteed, thinly-sliced bread, cut to any desired shape; or use thin, plain crackers).

HOT SHRIMP-CRAB SALAD

Serves 4

1 1/2 cups crab meat
1 cup shrimp, drained
1 cup diced celery
1 small onion, minced
1/2 medium green pepper, chopped
4 sprigs parsley, chopped
Salt to taste
Dash cayenne
2 tsp. Worcestershire
1 cup mayonnaise
3/4 cup soft bread crumbs
2 T. salad oil
Juice of 1/2 lemon

Rinse and devein cooked shrimp. Chop shrimp coarsely. Mix all ingredients except salad oil and crumbs. Rub oil on 4 large crab shells, clam shells, or small baking dishes. Add shrimp/crab mixture. Mix crumbs and oil. Sprinkle on top. Bake at 350° for about 25 minutes.

SOUPS

RED CRAB SOUP

Serves 8

1 doz. live crabs
1 large onion, chopped
1 tsp. thyme
1 28-oz. can whole tomatoes
2 qt. water
1/8 cup butter
1/8 cup oil
1 clove garlic, minced
1 bay leaf
1/4 tsp. cayenne
1 T. chopped parsley
Salt and pepper to taste

Wash the live crabs under a garden hose or a running tap. Kill crabs by boiling for 2 minutes. Place on tray for a few minutes till cool enough to handle. *Save all drippings.* Clean crabs (see Chapter 6). Remove appendages, keeping both the claws and the legs. Break bodies in half. In a large, heavy soup pot, saute the crab pieces in the oil. Add the drippings, garlic, onion, bay leaf, and cook five minutes. Add the tomatoes and cayenne and cook a few more minutes. Add the water, and simmer for 45 minutes, partially covered. Taste. Add salt and pepper as desired, parsley, and thyme. Remove claws and legs but not bodies, serve soup in bowls. Discard legs. Garnish each bowl with two claws, and a bit of fresh parsley. Diners can eat the meat within the crab bodies.

CAPE COD CRAB SOUP

Serves 6-8

2 cups crab meat
2/3 cup stale bread crumbs
1 slice onion
2 T. butter
Salt to taste
2 T. flour
3 cups chicken stock
(can be made with bouillon packets)
1 sprig parsley
1 cup half and half
Dash cayenne

Chop crab meat finely, and place in a heavy pot. Add stock or bouillon, crumbs, onion and parsley. Simmer 20 minutes. In separate saucepan, combine butter and flour until smooth. Add to first mixture. Add half and half. Season to taste. Garnish with fresh chopped dill if desired.

CHEESY CRAB SOUP

Serves 4-6

2 T. butter
1/4 tsp salt
1 qt. milk
Dash Tabasco
1 T. minced chives
2 T. flour
Dash pepper
1/2 lb. cheddar cheese
1 1/2 cups crab meat

Melt butter in saucepan. Stir in flour, salt and pepper. Gradually add milk. Cook over hot water, stirring constantly until thickened. Add diced cheese, stir until cheese melts. Add Tabasco. Add crab meat. Heat, garnish with chives.

MAIN DISHES

SPECIAL CRAB CASSEROLE

Serves 4

1/2 cup mild cheese, grated
1/2 cup sherry
3 T. butter
3 T. flour
3 cups crab meat
1/4 tsp. pepper
1 very small onion, chopped
1 small green pepper, chopped
2 eggs

In a saucepan, melt butter over low heat. Add onion and pepper, cook a few minutes. Sprinkle on the flour and cook thoroughly. Meanwhile, mix crab meat, eggs, cheese, sherry, pepper, and a little salt if desired. Blend the two mixtures. Fold into an oiled baking dish. Top with a little more cheese, and paprika. Bake about 12-15 minutes in a 375° oven.

MOM'S CREOLE

1 onion, chopped
2 T. butter
Dash each salt and pepper
1/2 tsp. Worcestershire
1 green pepper, chopped
1 19-oz. can tomatoes
  or stewed tomatoes
1 tsp. sugar or to taste
1 cup or more crab meat

Saute onions and pepper in butter for two or three minutes until soft. Add tomatoes and seasonings. Simmer about 10 minutes. Add crab meat only long enough to warm it. Serve over rice.
To make crab casserole creole: Place 1½ to 2 cups cooked rice in the bottom of a casserole dish. Pour over tomato mixture, then crab meat. Sprinkle ¼ cup grated cheese on top. Bake 20 minutes covered in a 350° oven. Uncover and bake 10 minutes more.

Try early and late in the season, even when people say "the crabs aren't running." Blue claws are notorious for making unusual early, late, or even "split" runs.

CRAB AND SHRIMP, DIXIE STYLE

1 small onion minced
3 T. flour
1/4 tsp. seasoned pepper
1/2 tsp. grated lemon rind
1 2/3 cup crab meat
3 T. butter or margarine
1 tsp. seasoned salt
1/2 tsp. steak sauce
1 1/2 cups milk
1/2 cup light cream
1 4 1/2-oz. can shrimp
(about 1 cup fresh chopped)
Hot biscuits

Cook onion in butter until golden. Blend in flour and seasonings. Add lemon rind, milk, and cream and cook, stirring, until thickened. Add crab and shrimp and heat. Season to taste and serve over piping hot biscuits.

CRAB FU YUNG

Serves 4

1 cup crab meat
1/2 cup shredded onion
3 T. oil
1 T. soy sauce
1 tsp. salt
Sauce (see below)
1 cup bean sprouts
1/2 cup finely sliced celery
6 eggs
1 T. cornstarch
Dash pepper

Place crab meat and sprouts in a large mixing bowl. If using canned sprouts, rinse and drain first. To cut onion in shreds, cut in half, from top to bottom. Then put on cutting board and finely slice with the grain. Saute onion and celery in oil until limp, about 5 minutes. Add to crab meat. Beat eggs, add soy sauce, cornstarch, salt and pepper. Pour over crab meat and vegetables and mix thoroughly. Ladle one T. of this mixture onto a greased griddle or skillet and brown. Turn and brown on other side. Keep warm in oven until all are cooked. Pour sauce over top.

Sauce for Crab Fu Yung: Cook until thick 1/2 cup water, 2 tsp. sherry, 1 T. soy sauce, and 2 tsp. cornstarch.

DEVILED CRAB #1

Serves 4

1 10 1/2 oz. can cream of celery soup
2 T. chopped green pepper
2 tsp. lemon juice
1 cup crab meat
1 T. chopped onion
1 tsp. Worcestershire
1/2 tsp. prepared mustard
  for baking

Combine all ingredients in a mixing bowl. Spoon into four shells or baking dishes. Sprinkle about 2 T. bread crumbs over each one. Bake about 20 minutes or until lightly browned, in a 350° oven.

DEVILED CRAB #2

Serves 6

4 cups lump crab meat
Juice of 1/4 lemon
1 hard-cooked egg, chopped
Bread crumbs
1/8 cup chopped chives
1 cup thick white sauce
1/2 tsp. Worcestershire
1/8 cup sherry
Butter
Paprika
1/4 cup mushrooms, chopped
1/2 tsp. dry mustard

Preheat oven to 450°. Grease 6 crab shells or a 2-qt. casserole. Combine crab meat and white sauce. Stir in mustard, lemon juice, sherry, chives, and eggs. Fill shells or casserole. Sprinkle with dry crumbs. Sprinkle with paprika, dot with butter. Bake in preheated oven for 15 minutes or until lightly browned.

CRAB QUICHE

2 T. minced onion
1 cup crab meat
Dash pepper
2 T. dry white wine
1 T. tomato paste
1 8-inch pastry shell
3 T. butter
Dash salt
1/4 cup grated swiss cheese
3 eggs
1 cup whipping cream

Cook the onion in butter until wilted, about 2 minutes. Add crab meat and stir for a few minutes. Add wine, raise heat, and boil for a few moments. Allow to cool slightly. Beat the eggs in a mixing bowl with the cream, tomato paste, and seasonings. Gradually blend in the crab meat. Pour mixture into pastry shell and sprinkle cheese over it. Bake in preheated 350° oven for 25-30 minutes, until quiche has puffed and browned. (Note: Shell should be baked for 10 minutes before filling so crust won't get soggy.)

CRAB MEAT MORNAY

2 cups crab meat
2 slices fresh bread
torn into pieces
Dry crumbs
1 T. butter
2 T. lemon juice
Mornay Sauce (below)

Mornay Sauce

2 cups medium-thick
white sauce
1/2 cup gruyere, grated
1 tsp. Worcestershire
2 T. butter
1/2 cup white wine if desired
1 tsp. prepared mustard
Salt and pepper to taste

Prepare white sauce. Stir in cheese, mustard, Worcestershire, salt and pepper. Cook over low heat, stirring constantly until cheese is melted. Remove from heat. Add butter, small pieces at a time, whisking well after each addition.

Master Recipe -
Preheat oven to 375°. Grease a 1 1/2 qt. casserole. Add crab meat. Top with lemon juice, then fresh bread pieces. Then top with the Mornay sauce. Dot with butter, and sprinkle on some dry crumbs. Bake for about 12 minutes or until golden.

CRAB OMELET

Serves 2

1 cup crab meat
4 eggs
Dash salt
2 T. butter
4 T. milk or cream
1/8 tsp. pepper

Beat eggs lightly. Add milk and seasonings. Put butter in hot omelet pan. Saute crab meat lightly. Fold in egg mixture.

Options - A wide variety of omelet ingredients can be added, as desired. These would include chopped green pepper or onion; asparagus tips, chopped; mushrooms; parsley; chopped or grated cheeses; diced tomato.

CRAB PILAF

Serves 6

1 T. butter
2 small onions, chopped fine
1 tsp. dry basil, crumbled
Salt and pepper to taste
2 T. chopped dill
3 T. tomato puree
1 T. oil
1 clove garlic, minced
2 ripe tomatoes, peeled, seeded, and chopped
1 1/2 cups dry white wine
4 cups crab meat
Pinch of sugar

Combine oil and butter in a saucepan. Saute garlic and onion lightly. Add the tomatoes and basil, and salt and pepper to taste. Cook over low heat until well blended. Stir in the tomato puree and the crab meat. Add the white wine, dill and sugar. Cook, stirring, until blended. Serve over cooked rice.

MARYLAND LADY CRAB CAKES

Makes 6 cakes

4 cups crab meat
Less than 1/4 cup mayonnaise
1 large egg
1/2 tsp. salt, or less
Half butter and half oil for frying
1 cup seasoned Italian bread crumbs
1 tsp. Worcestershire
1 tsp. dry mustard
1/4 tsp. black pepper, or less

Mix egg, mayonnaise, bread crumbs, and seasonings. Add crab meat and mix gently but thoroughly. If mixture is too dry, add a little more mayonnaise. Mixture should be just firm enough to shape into 6 crab cakes. Saute cakes in just enough butter and oil to prevent them from sticking. Cook about 5 minutes on each side.

CRAB SURPRISE

Serves 4

1 tsp. Worcestershire
2 eggs
8 oz. mild cheddar cheese, chopped
3 T. mayonnaise or salad dressing
1 cup milk
8 thin bread slices
1/4 tsp. salt
1 T. prepared mustard
1/2 cup diced celery
1 1/2 cups crab meat
1 cup milk

Combine celery and crab meat. Combine mayonnaise or salad dressing, mustard, and salt. Add this to crab mixture. Spread between the bread slices, making 4 sandwiches. Halve the sandwiches. Alternate layers of sandwich halves and cheese in a greased baking dish. Beat eggs; add milk and Worcestershire sauce to eggs. Pour over sandwiches. Bake at 325° for about 45 minutes.

CRABS CAPPY

2 large cloves garlic, very finely minced
2 med. green Italian peppers, chopped
28 oz. fresh tomatoes; weigh on scale. It will be 3-4 large ones. Or, use 1 28 oz.– can peeled, whole tomatoes.
Seasonings to taste. Approx. 1 T. sugar and 1 tsp. each of dried parsley, basil, oregano.
Dash of fresh pepper.
1 Med. onion, chopped
3 T. oil
1 T. butter
2 6-oz. cans tomato paste
1 can (1 lb. 12 oz) tomato puree or equivalent in prepared sauce
Water as needed (It will depend on the water content of the whole tomatoes.)
12 very large or 18 medium or 24 small crabs, live

Saute garlic in oil. Add butter. Add onions and saute over low flame until wilted and golden. Add paste and 1 cup water. Simmer, covered, for 15 minutes. Kill crabs in boiling water, about 2 minutes. Clean, then break crabs into pieces; wash, and place on a tray. Reserve *all* drippings while you do this. Add tomatoes and tomato puree, and drippings. Cook 30 minutes, skimming off any tough pieces or skin that might remain. When nearly smooth, add seasonings to taste. Add crab pieces. Add more water or paste to thin or thicken sauce as desired. Simmer over lowest flame for 1 1/2 to 2 hours. Serve over linguine. Notes: A heavy enamel or stainless steel pot is desirable. By all means use fresh herbs if available. If you do, use 3 times as much, more or less to taste. Serves 8 or more. Sauce will be much better the second day. Freezes very well. Use within six months.

OPEN CRAB SANDWICH DIVAN

Makes four open sandwiches

1/3 cup melted butter
1 cup shredded cheddar cheese or 1 cup grated parmesan
2 cups crab meat
1/3 cup mayonnaise
1 tsp. prepared mustard
Several spears broccoli
2 8-inch pieces french bread

Cut the bread lengthwise so you have four half sandwiches. Butter each piece lightly with melted butter. Place under the broiler for a few minutes until just golden. Remove. Combine mayonnaise and mustard. Spoon some of the flaked crab meat on each piece of bread. Top with the broccoli spears, and then the mayonnaise mixture. Sprinkle on the cheese and broil until the cheese is melted and starting to bubble. Serve hot.

CRAB AMANDINE

Serves 4

3 1/2 cups flaked crab meat
3 T. fresh parsley
1/2 cup sliced almonds
1/2 cup butter
4 large crab legs, cooked
1 large garlic clove,
  crushed with a garlic press
3 1/2 cups cooked rice
Salt to taste

Place almonds in a frying pan without butter. Stir over low heat, watching that the almonds do not burn. When lightly browned, remove almonds to dish. Oil a 1 1/2 qt. casserole. Place flaked crab meat in bottom. Melt butter in saucepan. Add garlic and parsley chopped fine, and stir for a few minutes. Add pepper and salt to taste. Pour this mixture over crab meat, then top with almonds. Arrange the crab legs around the perimeter of the casserole. Place under the broiler for five minutes, or bake at 400° for about 12 minutes. Serve over fluffy rice. Be sure to eat the meat in the crab legs.

DEEP-FRIED SOFTSHELL CRABS

Serves 6

12 softshell crabs
1 1/2 tsp. salt
3/4 cup flour
3/4 cup cracker meal
Parsley
Tartar sauce, if desired
1/4 tsp. pepper
Milk
2 eggs, lightly beaten
Fat for deep frying
Lemon wedges

Wash crabs under running water. Cut away mouth and eye parts. Pry open the apron of the crab, and remove all very soft materials (internal organs). Top shell can then be laid back into place. If you've never cleaned a softshell, let the man in the fish store show you how to do it once. Wipe crabs and dry with paper. Sprinkle crabs with salt and pepper. Soak in milk to cover for about 30 minutes. Drain crabs. Roll in flour. Dip in egg, then cracker meal. Fry in deep fat, heated to 365°, until crisp and golden. Drain on absorbent paper. Garnish with parsley and lemon wedges. Serve with tartar sauce if desired.

SOFTSHELL SAUTÉ FRANCAISE

Serves 2

Butter
Flour seasoned with
salt and pepper
2 T. dry white wine
4 softshell crabs
2 eggs, beaten
Juice of 1/2 lemon

Dredge crabs (cleaned as in preceding recipe) in seasoned flour. Dip in egg. Saute in lightly browned butter about 5 minutes per side or until nice and crisp. Add lemon juice and wine to the pan, to form a sauce. Bring to a simmer and serve. As with the preceding recipe, makes an excellent sandwich (hot or room temperature).

BROILED SOFTSHELLS

Eight medium sized softshells will serve four people if you also offer up some homemade coleslaw and crispy french fries. Dredge the cleaned crabs lightly in flour, then place on a flat pan. Combine 1/2 cup softened butter, 4 T. chopped fresh parsley, 1 T. chopped fresh dill, 2 tsp. paprika, and about 1 tsp. or less salt. Brush the crabs liberally with half this mixture. Broil about 4 minutes. Turn over and spread on remaining mixture. Broil another 4 minutes or until crisp. Serve with pan juices, tartar sauce, or dill sauce.

FOR THE GOURMET

BEIGNETS AU FROMAGE AVEC CRABE
(Cheese puffs with crab meat)

1/2 cup butter
1/2 cup white wine
1 tsp. salt
Pinch garlic powder
6 whole eggs
3 cups crab meat
1 tsp. fresh, chopped dill
1/2 cup water
1 1/2 cups flour
Pinch nutmeg
Pinch cayenne
1 cup imported gruyere
1 cup swiss emmenthaler
1 cup jarlsberg

Place butter, wine, salt, nutmeg, garlic powder and cayenne in saucepan and boil for two minutes. Add flour and keep on fire, mixing with a wooden spatula until the mixture loosens. Remove from fire and cool.
Transfer to a mixing bowl. Add whole eggs one at a time (you can blend by hand but the best way is with the dough hook attachment on a mixer or food processor.) Add shredded cheeses, crab meat, and dill and mix well. Drop small pieces from a teaspoon into deep fat heated to 360° and fry until golden.

SPECIAL CRAB FLORENTINE

Line a 2 qt. casserole with cooked, fresh spinach leaves. Cover with a sauce Mornay (see a previous recipe in this chapter). Place the above beignets on top of the sauce. Sprinkle lightly with Pernod. Place under the broiler for a few minutes.

Crab populations fluctuate dramatically. Don't moan about the bad years—take advantage of the good ones.

CRAB MEAT A L'INDIENNE

Serves 4

2 cups light or heavy cream
Handful of blonde raisins
3 cups cooked rice
Juice of 1/2 lemon
2 T. butter
1 cup crab meat
1 tart apple
1 T. mild curry powder
1 tsp. chutney
1 banana
1 oz. cognac
Toasted coconut

Melt butter in a saucepan. Stir in curry powder. Add crab meat, saute lightly. Add cognac, light with a match. After flame subsides, add diced apple, banana and raisins. Add lemon juice and cream, cooking until thick. Meanwhile, with a round mold make a ring with the rice. Place crab mixture in middle. Sprinkle with toasted coconut.

SAUTEED SOFTSHELLS WITH FORTUNE SAUCE

12 softshell crabs
1 1-lb. can sliced peaches
Fortune sauce
Fresh dill
1/4 cup sliced, toasted almonds

Fortune Sauce -

1 T. butter, melted
2 T. flour
1 tsp. mild curry powder
1 cup half and half
1 T. dried dill or
  2 T. fresh, chopped dill
2 T. (more or less)
  of the crab cooking water

Whisk flour into melted butter in a heavy skillet. Add curry powder, blend well. Add the half and half, dill and juice from the can of peaches. Add 2 T. more or less of the crab cooking water a *little at a time*, cooking slowly until a thick sauce consistency is reached.

Master Recipe -
Saute the softshells a la the previous recipe, "Softshell Saute Francaise". Arrange them while still very warm in a deep serving dish. Cover with Fortune Sauce, then thinly sliced peaches from the can. Sprinkle with fresh chopped dill, and lightly sauted almond slices. Serve on rice if desired, along with a good loaf of Baquette bread. Note: Fortune Sauce can be used in many other seafood dishes. It can also be used, in place of melted butter, for dipping fresh-out-of-the-shell crab meat.

ROYAL CRAB SAUTE

Serves 4-6

4-5 scallions, chopped
1/2 lb. mushrooms, sliced
1 cup extra dry vermouth
(Noilly Prat)
Juice of 1 lime
Pinch of mild curry powder
Salt to taste
1 clove garlic, crushed
18 small softshell crabs, cleaned
1 large, ripe tomato: peeled,
cored, and coarsely chopped
1/4 cup whipped cream cheese
1 cup heavy cream
1/4 cup butter
1/4 cup flour
Pinch cayenne
Pinch paprika

Stir-fry scallions, garlic, tomatoes and mushrooms in butter in a large, heavy kettle for 2-3 minutes. Whisk in the flour until smooth. Simmer 2 or 3 more minutes. Add crabs. In a mixing bowl, whip the cream cheese with the vermouth, lime juice and heavy cream. Add this to the kettle a little at a time until smooth. Add spices to taste. Simmer 10 to 15 minutes longer. Serve with green salad and potato pancakes.

BLUE CLAW CRABS À LA OLIVIER

Serves 2-3

6 large, hardshell crabs
1 cup olive oil
Salt and pepper to taste
3 cloves garlic
1 cup fresh parsley

Boil crabs for 15 minutes. Remove claws and clean crabs. Mince finely the parsley and garlic. Whisk these into olive oil, add salt and pepper. Align crab bodies in a deep dish, open side up. While crab bodies are still warm, pour the oil mixture over them. As oil and crab juices mix together in the bottom of the dish baste them back over crabs. Good when served cold.